East of San Diego

The Lost History of the East San Diego

Police Department

1912 –1923

GARY E. MITROVICH

San Diego Police Historical Association

East of San Diego: The Lost History of the East San Diego
Police Department

Published by:
  The San Diego Police History Association
  San Diego, California
  www.sandiegopolicemuseum.com

ISBN 978-0-0708501-0-3

printed in the United States of America

This small bit of San Diego history
is dedicated to my children

Alex and Kayla

And to the rest of my family

Contents

Acknowledgements

History encompasses everything that has occurred before this very moment. That's a lot of stuff. While much of history is interesting, most of history is quite trivial and eventually fades away forever. What amazes me is how quickly memories disappear. This little segment of local history transpired less than a century ago, yet there is little left to see or research. Fortunately, I had a lot of help in my hunt for information.

I began this research in the mid-nineties (the 1990's) with a very general three-page article on this subject. Thanks to Gwen Gunn, friend and editor of The Informant (the Official Publication of the San Diego Police Officers Association) for printing that story (and many others I wrote about local history).

The San Diego Police Historical Association deserves endless appreciation, as this book simply would not have happened without them. Thank you to the Board of Directors for their support, with special notice to Ed Austin, Steve Rosenbloom, and Steve Willard for their encouragement and assistance.

Additionally, former San Diego Police Historical Association Commissioner Vonn Marie May provided me much guidance and support as I began my project.

Thanks to Ann Jarmusch of the San Diego Union as well.

The San Diego Historical Society must be commended for maintaining local history. Without access to the East San Diego Press newspaper, this would have been a very short work indeed. The information in the East San Diego Press is valuable beyond measure, documenting a time and a place that is documented by little else in existence. Additionally, the always kind and uncomplaining workers in the San Diego Historical Society's archives must also be recognized. I truly appreciate their endless patience and assistance. I spent many hours in their basement and they never failed to make me feel welcome.

My thanks to the folks in the California Room of the San Diego Public Library, who are always thoughtful and obliging, and to the City of San Diego Clerk's Office, who provided me copies of the few official documents still on file concerning East San Diego.

The City of Coronado Public Library was accommodating beyond expectation – especially Ms. Susan Hayman, who researched the Frank Hyatt family in Coronado and uncovered a number of interesting newspaper articles on my behalf.

Special thanks to Patty Rank, the granddaughter of the first Chief of Police for the City of East San Diego. I found her a wonderful and fascinating person and am truly thankful for her help. I also want to express gratitude to Rae McHorney, surviving daughter of East San Diego's last city marshal, Nat McHorney. Rae donated a priceless album to our San Diego Historical Association, filled with wonderful photographs and documents.

My parents — Harold and Loretta Mitrovich — both provided support and input with their own experiences as natives of San Diego. My son, Alex, accompanied me on many an expedition and contributed with photographs and companionship.

Finally, I want to thank my late grandparents, Nick and Dorothy Mitrovich, who both grew up in San Diego and sparked my own interested in local history with first-hand stores of their own.

Introduction

As history goes, most people know that San Diego began in Old Town. But the city didn't really start growing until it moved its civic center (literally, in the middle of the night) to what they called New Town—today's Downtown area. Only then did a succession of land booms hit town and, with each exciting ebb and disappointing flow, San Diego really started to grow as a city.

As the downtown core grew, other settlements started to appear in the outer regions of the county. It's hard to believe that, little more than 100 years ago, many of San Diego's communities were like outposts of humanity surrounded by desolate and undeveloped acres. Connected by dirt roads and some streetcar rails, the impetus for these settlements was somewhat varied. Some towns birthed in the search for precious metal, others sprang forth to support the farming of fruits and vegetables. Mostly though, communities were borne of population growth and the need for housing.

One such community holds a unique place in local history—the community once and again know as City Heights. For a short but tumultuous 11 years in the early

20th Century, that suburb was incorporated as the City of East San Diego.

Separate and apart from its older and larger neighbor, East San Diego existed as a separate municipality from 1912 to 1923. During its lifetime, ESD elected its own mayor and city council (referred to as their President and Board of Trustees). These bodies, in turn, appointed officials to conduct the various functions of a city. One such function was of paramount importance —the function of law enforcement.

Though they called their first appointee the Chief of Police, ESD had decided to proceed with the city marshal system, probably because it was less expense than forming a formal police department. The procedure went something like this: The Board of Trustees would appoint a man who would serve at their leisure. The city marshal would appoint deputies as required. As a rule, the top cop would then change with each succeeding administration. Such constant turnover often resulted in a lack of consistency and low morale. The City of San Diego had moved away from this system and created their own police department 25 years before, but grappled with the same turnover of Chiefs until a major City Charter change in the early 1930's created more stability in the leadership.

While most ESD city records are unaccounted for and may forever be lost to posterity, it appears the first few city marshals had no regular police force to speak of. They may have simply appointed deputies as needed. As ESD grew and experienced associated pains, the need for more cops became apparent, especially in regard to traffic enforcement. A night watchman was later added, as well as "speed" cops and motorcycle officers to slow

Clearing brush for the New City Heights streets, also known as "grubbing." In 1906, the relatively flat mesa east of Downtown was little more than sagebrush and rocks. San Miguel Mountain looms in the background.

down traffic and save lives. In later years, the City Marshal and even the local newspaper would start referring to its lawmen as their "police department."

Additionally, the city had a justice of the peace assigned to the "Mission Township." Judge A.A. Schilling employed a court constable, who eventually became a vital ally to the city marshal. However, the County Board of Supervisors eliminated the township assignment at the end of 1918.

When East San Diego began in 1912, the town boasted a population of some 4,000. When it consolidated with the City of San Diego in 1923, ESD's population had grown to 12,000 people. And, as its residents transitioned to a new city, a few law officers joined the new city's police department.

Historical research is quite literally traveling into the past. After each research expedition, I felt I had taken a trip back through time. By reading the style of the time and seeing the photos, I stepped through a portal of adventure. It was almost disappointing to have to return to the present.

The *East San Diego Press* newspaper was my time machine and I am thankful for its existence. While many issues are (frustratingly) missing, it served as a rare and somewhat detailed history of a city that once was. The San Diego Historical Society should be proud they have preserved and made available such a valuable resource. Simply, this book could not have been possible with it.

My goal is always to give an exhaustive and complete account of my chosen subject. However, history is often a nasty little tease. While facts can often suggest and point the way, conclusions can often be in short supply. So the researcher becomes involved in a tricky little game of "connect the dots." Great care must be taken in this endeavor. Reasonable speculation is valuable and even necessary in historical research, but only if such guesswork is clearly framed and identified. Too many authors have allowed their egos to convince themselves that they know enough to make such interpretation without sharing that fact with their readers. I shall not do this. And I will welcome alternate views and deductions.

I have some high aspirations for my little history book (as do most authors). I truly hope this volume educates (yes—not a bad word) and even entertains. But even more so, my hope is this report might lead to other information, records, memories, etc. I hope family members and others who know more about the City of East San Diego —especially the law enforcement aspect—read this manuscript and contact me. I look forward to it. I plan to publish an updated, 2nd edition. Won't you help out?

City Heights and the
City of East San Diego

O nce upon a time, there was the City of East San Diego. It sprang from the seed of expansion and grew slowly on a mesa some 400 feet in elevation and seven miles northeasterly from Downtown San Diego. This is its story:

In 1888, San Diego was in the midst of a great land boom. In less than a year's time, the population had swelled from roughly 6,000 to (by some estimates) over 40,000. As lots sold like hot cakes, what was called "New Town" began to bulge and expand outward. Speculators immediately eyed the surrounding open lands as unmined gold. Local visionary Abraham Klauber[1] recognized the value of a relatively flat and undeveloped mesa northeast of downtown. He led an entrepreneurial troupe in the purchase 240-plus acres there. Legally known as the Steiner, Klauber, Choate[2] and Castle Addition, the community was christened "City Heights."

[1] Klauber was a Czech immigrant who settled in San Diego in 1869. He bought several lots from Alonzo Horton and partnered with Samuel Steiner to open a general merchandising store at 7th and "I" Streets.
[2] Daniel Choate rivaled Alonzo Horton as the largest operator in early San Diego real estate.

A view from the fifth floor of the City Heights Tower in 1910, the streetcar tracks split University Avenue below, still a dirt road. The nearest cross street is 43rd, then called Pauly Street.

The establishment of the Park Belt Motor Line railroad in July 1888 meant that citizens and—even more importantly—prospective *buyers* could travel to the new community on one of three daily trains. Newspaper advertisements proclaimed the new rail line to be "the most substantially built, the most expensive, picturesque and…cheapest ride of any motor road in San Diego." The little-known railroad loop started at the intersection of 18th (site of Interstate 5) and "A" Streets, then proceeded northeasterly through present-day City Shops and into Switzer Canyon, under 30th Street (a bridge at the time) and finally onto University Avenue.

As if more enticement were required, City Heights was touted as a place for "cheap homes" and "monthly

A community icon for decades, the City Heights Tower originally stood on the south side of University Avenue, mid-block between 43rd Street and Fairmount Avenue. Built in 1906 to serve the Columbia Realty Company, the lumber for the five-story tower was said to have cost $1500. The tower was moved across the street in 1912.

payments" with "no interest." The new community was now primed for its own land boom.

And boom it did. The new development attracted instant interest and sales were brisk. Even Wyatt Earp bought a lot in Teralta (i.e., "high land"), a neighborhood very near City Heights. A San Diego resident at the time, Earp and his wife had come to town with many other boomers. Only seven years before, the former lawman had been in a little gunfight over in Tombstone, Arizona Territory. Here, Earp cashed in on the boom and bought property from the border to Hillcrest. In Teralta, he purchased a property on Swift

A single streetcar track splits University Avenue on the dirt street. In 1910, the eastern terminus was Fairmount Avenue. Several years later, the track would be extended to Euclid Avenue, where streetcars would end their eastward travels until the entire system was abruptly abandoned in 1949.

Avenue for $200 in June 1888. He never developed the land, it but held onto it until 1895, when he sold it for a mere $2.

When San Diego's boom went bust and the population fell drastically (to about 17,000), City Heights suffered its own bust. The Park Belt Line went belly-up and, though land was owned, few improvements were made to the sagebrush-covered community.

John Spreckels injected new life into the area with his bold ideas for San Diego. In 1905, Spreckels announced plans to extend his San Diego Electric Trolley Company onto University Avenue and into City Heights. He also planned an ambitious transcontinental railroad line for the region. Those proposals, along with the news of the proposed Panama Canal, triggered another real estate boom in San Diego.

Another look at the tower in 1910. Potential real estate investors would climb the five stories to the top for a visual survey of the new community. In 1910, a total of 475 homes dotted the little community. By contrast, only three houses stood in the area just four years earlier.

By 1906, the Columbia Realty Company owned much of City Heights. The Company felt so encouraged they re-platted their subdivision to prepare for upcoming development. Anticipating an "eastside streetcar suburb," Columbia built a five-story tower on the south side of University Avenue at Fairmount.[3] It served as both an end-of-the-line streetcar attraction and a platform for prospective developers to climb upon and envision their dreams.

Development was still a little slow in coming, but it soon gathered speed. While Columbia Realty reported only

[3] That tower was later moved across the street to the north side of University Avenue, where it remained until 1939.

Emma Schnug residence in 1910, perhaps the oldest house in East San Diego

three City Heights homes in 1907, there were 50 by 1908, 150 the following year, and some 475 homes by 1910. In fact, the *San Diego Union* reported City Heights was experiencing a steady increase in residential and commercial development. In 1911, Oscar Cotton and his Pacific Building Company purchased and began to develop the Fairmount Addition, east of City Heights.

It rained heavily on November 2, 1912. As a result, only 500 of the 836 registered voters in City Heights made it to the polls. The final tally was 288 for and 212 against. Though it was big news for the little city, the results were small potatoes in the big city. Buried way back on page seven, the *San Diego Union* rather matter-of-factly proclaimed that City Heights had incorporated by a majority vote of 76.

City Heights, also known as Teralta, was now the City of East San Diego. Officially incorporated on November 7, 1912, the boundaries were described as adjoining the eastern city limits of San Diego (at Boundary Street —which was appropriate), between El Cajon Boulevard and the Chollas Valley south. Its initial population of 4,000 was spread over six square miles, instantly making East San Diego the second largest city in the county. Plans were quickly formulated to throw off the "reins of county government" by the first of the New Year.

The Pacific Building Company took out this full-page advertisement in the December 1, 1912 "Sunday Morning" edition of the San Diego Union. Not even a month old, the City Of East San Diego was being heavily publicized.

East San Diego was now the largest city of its age in the whole of the United States, a fact its citizens enjoyed sharing with others. With an attitude that seemed to surpass pride, the city fathers quickly established a high moral bar that some perceived as arrogant. Instead of a mayor and city council, ESD would have a President and a Board of Trustees, all serving without pay (at least initially). Another haughty appearance was the establishment of an "Improvement Committee." Leaders soon adopted the official city motto: "Do unto others as you would that they do unto you." They called themselves the Golden Rule City.

It was clear that many had wanted to start their own city so as to control the kinds of businesses and actions that might be allowed there. Many activities were quickly prohibited and city leaders often touted their prohibition.

Forbidden in East San Diego were liquor sales or gifts, gambling, dance halls, the carrying of firearms, and horse hitching on University Avenue, the city's main street. Additionally, the speed limit could not exceed 15 miles per hour (for both horse and horseless carriages).

In its premiere issue of 1913, the *San Diego Union* highlighted East San Diego with a section of its very own. The good news included such facts as:

1. Not a pauper or public charity subject in the city
2. Has no jail
3. City has no arrests
4. No hoboes.

Of course it would fall mostly upon local law enforcement to maintain these high standards set by the city fathers.

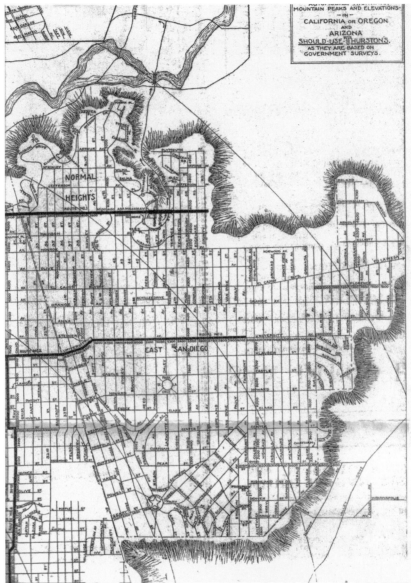

A rare map of the City of East San Diego in 1915. The neighboring communities to the north—Normal Heights and Kensington—were unincorporated county lands at this time.

The First Chief:
Justice Comes to East San Diego

Charles W. Justice: November 1912(?) To February 1913(?)
Born: March 17, 1872 (Downey, California)
Died: October 21, 1960 (San Diego, California)

With its incorporation, East San Diego announced the marshal position was to be an appointed one. Compensation for the position would be "affixed on a salary and fee basis." This was a common practice of the time, as the city marshal was usually the tax collector as well. The attraction was that the marshal usually earned a percentage of the taxes he collected. East San Diego would use this system until about 1915, when they separated the duties (for reasons currently unknown—it is possible that as the city and its tax base grew, the opportunity and the financial means became feasible).

"C.W. Justice" was appointed the first Chief of Police[1] of the City of East San Diego. In its full-page profile of

---

[1] It is interesting that the City fathers referred to their first top cop as "Chief of Police," possibly another example of the haughty aspirations of the city. All those following in Justice's footsteps were thereafter called the City Marshal.

Courtesy of Patty Rank

Charles W. Justice in front of his Mission Beach home at 817 Vanitie Court in the summer of 1954. Appointed the first "Chief of Police" for the City of East San Diego, his tenure was short-lived and he only served a few months.

East San Diego (January 1, 1913), the *San Diego Union* identified Justice as hailing from the Great State of Texas. While Justice was probably appointed prior to this date, this *Union* issue was his first official listing.[2] Unfortunately, the procedure and/or process for this selection may be forever lost to posterity.

Charles W. Justice was actually a native of the Golden State. He and his family had lived for a time in Texas — one of his sisters was born there—but this Justice was born in Downey, California. He attended the University of California at Los Angeles and, from about 1908 to 1912, was a member of the State Highway Commission.

The Justice family itself had arrived in San Diego in 1867. His father, William Justice (1843-1930), distinguished himself as an early San Diego County Supervisor. Brother John (1870-1959) and son Roy B. (1910-1970) also served civic duty locally. Roy spent over 40 years with the city.

Justice was 40 years old at the time of his appointment, but not much else is known of his tenure as Chief of Police. He and his family resided at 3862 Highland Avenue, though his occupation was listed as a simple "laborer."

---

[2] The first official listing that survives, that is.

Justice more than likely oversaw the investigation of one of East San Diego's first serious crimes: an attempted murder. It seems one Herman Bergstadt had been recently "released" from work at the Painless Dental Parlor. He protested this action by shooting the dentist, H.S. Welch, as the tooth doctor stepped from a streetcar at University Avenue and Pauly (43rd) Street. Welch survived his wounds and Bergstadt went to jail.

As Justice had no law enforcement experience before or after his stint in East San Diego, it is possible the job just sounded better in theory than in practice. Or maybe he got a better offer. To be certain, his tenure was short. After only a few months, Justice had resigned as Chief of Police to become the Supervisor of Streets for the City of San Diego. The exact date of and reason for his resignation is, unfortunately, unknown.

By 1915, Justice had moved to Point Loma and onto a different job ("teamster" for the street department). Family survivors were recently surprised to learn that Justice had been the debut law enforcement officer of little-known East San Diego. They speculate that Justice may have found himself in an untenable financial situation. He had two small children and—quite probably—a low paying job. His years of experience with the State Highway Commission made his a natural choice for the street department. Additionally, the City of San Diego may have owned that house on Point Loma, another financial factor. He remained in city employment for 32 years.

Family described Justice as a rugged man and a good writer. He may have thought so little of his time as Chief of Police that he felt it never needed mention. Or maybe

Credit: Steve Willard

Circa 1917, a sign posted at an unknown location some 10 miles from East San Diego. The Auto Club of Southern California posted many such signs to assist automobile motorists as they navigated new roads in the county.

he didn't feel his achievement was worthy of any attention. Justice died in his Mission Beach home at the age of 88. He was survived by two sons, two daughters, three sisters, and two grandchildren.[3]

---

[3] In 1974, granddaughter Patty Rank became one of the first female firefighters in San Diego and the United States.

City Marshal F. A. Hyatt

Frank A. Hyatt: March 1913 to June 1914
Born: June 13, 1844 (Ohio)
Died: January 27, 1941 (San Bernardino, California)

By March 1913, there was a new marshal in town. No longer would the position be referred to as "Chief of Police"—it was now the "City Marshal." And 68-year-old F.A. Hyatt had been appointed to succeed C.W. Justice.

Frank A. Hyatt must have been an interesting man. He was born before the Civil War and may have been somewhat of a wandering soul, as well as a man of many occupations. In 1870 he was living in Wisconsin with his first wife, Jennie. In 1871, his eldest child, Elizabeth, was born in Iowa, as was his oldest son Charles S.G. in 1873. The family moved to Colorado, where Wynona M. (1882) and George Francis (1893) were born. Frank most commonly listed his occupation as a "painter," though his law enforcement career seems to have started there.

Frank's first wife apparently passed away sometime after 1900 and by 1904 he was living alone in Coronado. During this time, Frank met his second "Jennie." In 1912,

Frank married Jennie M. Bazier of East San Diego in a quiet ceremony in the Coronado home of his niece and nephew, Mr. & Mrs. Frank Myers of 235 "C" Avenue. That union may have prompted his move to East San Diego soon thereafter—the 1913 San Diego City/County Directory shows Frank and Jennie residing at 3829 Van Dyke Street in ESD.

Frank Hyatt was probably a comfortable choice for the new municipality, perhaps reeling after losing its first top cop only months into cityhood. He had prior law enforcement experience as the Under Sheriff of Conejos, Colorado in 1885. And while living in Coronado, that City Directory listed him as a "private detective." The Tax Collector as well, Frank's salary was listed at $110 per month. He had at least one deputy, George A. DeBarrow,[1] and probably appointed others as necessary. The city was apparently solvent enough to approve the expansion of his Tax Collector's office, so Frank was able to appoint Miss Bessie Seay[2] to serve as his deputy tax collector[3].

Frank Hyatt's exact date of appointment to the office of City Marshal is not known. Per the *East San Diego Press* newspaper, he was up and running by March 1913.

Marshal Hyatt seemed to have enough to keep busy, with both the citizenry and the elected officials. The newspaper reported "Mr. Hyatt" had to be called in to preserve order at a Board of Trustees meeting in which a member of the Board of Health was to be dismissed. When one J.W Ingram rose to address the mayor "in words which were more forceful that politer," the mar-

---

[1] DeBarrow would be a city marshal candidate himself in 1914.
[2] Miss Seay's brother Clarence founded the second newspaper of East San Diego, *The Sentinel*.
[3] The appointment went effective on October 1, 1913.

shal was asked to interject. Frank requested "quiet on the part of Mr. Ingram," and the disturbance was settled. Ingram was then voted out.

Days later, the marshal was embroiled in a controversy that erupted with the headline, "Bradt Street House Raided." The *East San Diego Press* reported that, after a Board of Trustees meeting:

"President Holleman, City Attorney Welch, Trustees Hobson and Mayer, accompanied by Marshall [sic] Hyatt and Deputy DeBarrow, and some interested citizens, made a raid on an alleged house of ill repute on Bradt (Cherokee) Street and arrested three women and five men."

Though two of the women were eventually charged with serving intoxicating liquor, the others were released. The ESD Improvement Committee objected to the manner in which the raid was handled and a testy town meeting followed. Their main concern was negative publicity they claimed resulted (something ESD was very sensitive to), as the information was pre-released to the news media. Marshal Hyatt weathered the storm, but President Holleman and Trustee Mayer both resigned from their offices.

In a bizarre footnote to that event, the beer seized from Bradt Street was used by City Trustees to "christen" their new City Hall building the following week. Even more humorous was which City Hall was chosen to receive the honor. The actual, freshly constructed municipal building looked too much like a bungalow for the pride and taste of the Board, so another more stately structure was chosen to stand in for City Hall. The concern was that photographs of the event might make their way back east and cause some embarrassment to ESD.

Additionally, someone reported that a beer had gone missing. The culprit was never identified, but this was disturbing news in the "dry" town.

In July 1913, Hyatt charged the city for telephone usage and badges — $4.15 —and received a $25 salary. The style of those badges, and their current whereabouts, remain a mystery.

The City Heights Tower had become the Waffle Café by 1927. The upper floors were removed in 1936. The entire building was torn down in 1939.

Later in July, the marshal investigated a burglary at George H. Hall's store on El Cajon Boulevard.[4] The loss was $40 worth of cigars and chewing gum. Hyatt "hustled forth" and found the property in a shed at Pauly (43rd) Street and Orange Avenue. He deputized James Holgate and R.L. Green and then ordered them to sleep on the back porch of a neighboring cottage to watch over the woodshed. At 2 a.m. the following morning, an "automobile" drove up to the shed. A man got out and began to saw away at the new padlock placed on the shed. Deputy Marshal Green fired three shots at the suspect, who "raced wildly away; disappearing in the darkness." The deputies later discovered the car left behind had been stolen the previous day.

[4] Alternately referred to as an "Avenue" and a "Road." Early in the 20th Century, the street was even called "La Mesa Road." In 1926, the boulevard was classified as U.S Highway 80, part of the "Broadway of America" southern transcontinental highway route. This before the existence of interstate freeways, it explains the number of old motels along the road.

Frank Hyatt's tenure lasted throughout 1913 and into the following year. He reportedly fell seriously ill in April 1914 and was confined to his home for over two weeks. His term as city marshal came to an end shortly thereafter, though his service as a lawman would be tapped again.

After only several years together, Frank and Jennie apparently separated and lived at different residences. Frank later lived both with son Charles (who was a painter by 1915) and son George. By 1918, Jennie had moved to San Diego and was last listed there in 1921. The 1920 United States Census lists both Frank and Jennie as "widowed," apparently a reference to the former spouse of each. Later, when Frank moved to San Bernardino, he was living with daughter Elizabeth and her husband.

Son Charles S.G. Hyatt had his own law enforcement career, albeit a short one. He joined the San Diego Police Department on January 15, 1912. In his 2½ years with SDPD, he served as a patrolman, detective, inspector, and mounted patrolman. By the time he resigned on September 28, 1914, Charles was once again a patrolman.

The other son, George Francis (1893-1972) AKA "Buck," dabbled in law enforcement as well. In 1918, newly appointed ESD city marshal William H. Gray appointed the younger Hyatt as one of his deputies. Buck was also serving as the ESD city engineer at the time, a post he left in September 1918 for a similar one in the City of Coronado. Often (and confusingly) referred to as "Frank" Hyatt, Buck promoted to Coronado's City Manager in January 1920. He was often commended as having "a wisdom matured beyond his own years and an enthusiasm that can spell nothing but success." He served that city until his resignation in July 1923.

In December 1915, Frank Hyatt was identified as a deputy city marshal in the *East San Diego Press.* In October 1917, County Sheriff Conklin stopped by ESD to appoint Hyatt as a deputy sheriff. Frank was called upon to assist at the County Jail, where a young man by the name of Sloan was being held for the murder of a chauffer in Oceanside. Hyatt apparently knew the accused and his family from his Colorado days. The reporter expounded: "For 22 years, Mr. Hyatt was sheriff of Conejo County, Colorado, and that was during the stirring times of some years ago, so he is well versed in the business." The same article indicated Hyatt was still serving as an ESD deputy marshal.

Hyatt embarked on another career in ESD, one in which many of his peers also indulged: real estate. Born of a land boom, ESD was all about property. In 1917, during one particular lull in land sales, Frank heard that folks thought he kept his real estate office open as a joke. An apparent optimist, Hyatt's response was, "just wait until conditions revive, then I'll show some of those smart guys a thing or two." The land picture did improve and by 1918, Frank had established a real estate office with Zenas Freeman. It was one of dozens of such businesses sprinkled throughout East San Diego. From 1920 to 1923, Hyatt apparently operated the office on his own.

Frank eventually retired and moved to San Bernardino. He died there in 1941, at the age of 96.

Constables of the Court

There was another arm of law enforcement in East San Diego back in the day. In addition to the City Marshal and his deputies, there was the Constable of the Justice Court.

The constable was a throwback to Old England, where the office originated and continues today. In the United States, the office existed in colonial times, but was altered as the modern police force developed. Today, there is no consistent use of the title in this country. In fact, the constable grows scarce as time marches on.

As for East San Diego, the constable acted as a sworn officer for the local Justice Court, much the same as the marshals formerly (and now sheriff's deputies) serve courtrooms today. It's interesting that, as the constable has passed out of vogue, so did the justice courts.

The California State Constitution of 1849 authorized justice courts. As counties were divided into judicial townships, each township was allowed two justices of the peace. An elected position, the justice's jurisdiction was limited to their township.

These courts initially heard some civil and misdemeanor cases. State statutes allowed civil jurisdiction to include recovery of contract money, damages, or rulings on disputed property, as well as mortgage foreclosures. Criminal jurisdiction covered petty theft, assault and battery cases, disturbing the peace, and other misdemeanors that did not exceed certain fine or imprisonment levels.

By 1914, Andrew A. Schilling was serving ESD as city recorder and justice of the peace. He was elected to the Mission Township, Department Number One, which apparently encompassed most if not all of East San Diego. Schilling would serve in this office until it passed out of existence.

One of the first constables mentioned in the *East San Diego Press* was Harold J. Slease. In April 1913, Constable "H.G." Slease (a probable typographical error) arrested one Louis Onetervera for a warrant charging the man with shooting at a horse owned by Metilla Gonzales. Apparently, there was some sort of ongoing feud between the Onetervera and Gonzales families, as similar shooting incidents had apparently occurred. Justice of the Peace George B. Keith released the accused on $2 bail. The case was scheduled for trial the following day, at Fairmount Hall on Pauly (43rd) Street. Onetervera was tried and acquitted by Judge Keith.

Slease hailed from Ohio, born in 1876. A shoemaker by trade, he and his wife Alice had settled in City Heights prior to its incorporation. By about 1915, Slease had moved his family to New Mexico. He died in Phoenix, Arizona in 1946, at the age of 70.

Charles F. Rapp served as a "deputy constable" in 1915. Rapp was a New York native born in 1879. A retail merchant before coming to California, Rapp was also a skilled carpenter. By 1930, he was the Postmaster for the City of

La Mesa. Rapp was married and had three children. He died in 1953, while still residing in San Diego.

William M. Tompkins was another of the many transplanted New Yorkers who eventually made their home in East San Diego. He was an attorney who served as "Chief Deputy Constable" in 1916. Tompkins married his wife in East San Diego and fathered a son in 1916. He passed away suddenly in September 1931.

Far and away, the most popular constable that served East San Diego was C.E. "Bunny" Murray. Murray was a well known, oft quoted, and civic-minded individual. He and wife Mae lived in the city during its early years. In 1914, Murray was among the half dozen or so initial candidates for the City Marshal position. While the Board of Trustees passed on that application, they evidently thought enough of the man to appoint him city treasurer. The *East San Diego Press* poked a little fun at Murray when they claimed that, "City Treasurer Murray can sometimes be found at city hall."

While it is not known exactly when Murray took over the office, the 1916 San Diego City and County Directory lists "C Edmund Murray" as constable, residing in the City of East San Diego. He stirred up a hornet's nest later that year.

One of the bullet points on which East San Diego liked to brag was the fact they had no city jail. That wasn't to say people didn't get arrested (though they did brag, in a city advertisement, that there were no arrests in their fair city). Arrestees that needed detainment and or imprisonment were shipped off to the county jail. Murray had the audacity to suggest (via communiqué to city trustees) that ESD could use a jail of its own, "for the keeping of all

The Presbyterian Church was built at Pauly and Anna Streets. It still stands on the northwest corner of 43rd Street and Polk Avenue. The parish constructed the pastor's house in a similar design several lots north (another house that remains today).

law violators." To that end, he had tentatively identified a free source of lumber (that source being the county, provided the city pay for the initial labor and upkeep). City fathers tabled the issue.

When the *East San Diego Press* got hold of the information, they had a little field day at Murray's expense. "Is Constable C.E. Murray trying to ruin East San Diego's reputation?" asked the Page One article. Though they complimented him as "one of our capable peace officers," the tabloid wondered what Murray meant "by trying to place East San Diego in such a bad light with other decent and law abiding communities."

"Don't you remember, Mr. Constable, that while you were holding down the position of city treasurer that you wrote the check which paid an advertising bill for an ad which appeared in a magazine telling the world that East San Diego had no jails, saloons or graveyards?"

The diatribe continued sarcastically, questioning if "Mr. Constable" would "be in favor of ruining a record which is held by no other city in the world" (whatever that particular record might be). The reporter bragged (an ESD pastime) that there had never been more than a dozen arrests in any one year since the city's inception. Finally, the paper went on the record to disagree with the need for a city jail—though they indicated they might support a graveyard.

The issue died on the table. It would be brought up again some years later, by a different lawman, with much less fanfare and opposition.

Murray seemed quick to support and assist city marshals whenever they required him. He was in on the raid of a "questionable house" in the 4400 block of Estrella Avenue. He testified in the slander case of a former city trustee versus prominent leaders of the East San Diego Civic League, though little of his testimony was allowed. When the city purchased several "dummy policemen" (automatic traffic towers installed at busy intersections to regulate the flow of traffic), Murray threw his support behind the plan.

In August 1917, the *East San Diego Press* ran a detailed article regarding the efforts of the city marshal's office. Murray's name figured prominently. Not only was he credited for closing the notorious "pink house" (a den of alcohol and prostitution iniquities), he received a heartfelt commendation from the newspaper: "Special credit should be given to the constable of the Mission township, C.E. Murray (also known as 'catch em' Murray) and to the district attorney's office, for their constant cooperation."

The beginning of 1918 found Murray was recovering Jose Alvetrio's stolen horse from Ellen Young, by order of

Credit: San Diego Historical Society

University Avenue served as the main street of East San Diego. The avenue had been "double-tracked" by this time, circa 1917. Rueben Quartermass built the large house facing Fairmount Avenue in 1906-07. Charles Stensrud bought the house and the City Heights Tower behind it in 1912. New owners moved the house to 56th Street and Adams Avenue in 1929, where it stands today.

Judge Keating. At the same time, he was advocating (perhaps tongue-in-cheek) the killing of all worthless dogs and cats, an act he felt "would help the government win the war." Murray added that either he or Marshal Ayers would be pleased to exterminate a wayward pet, at the behest of the stray's owner.

In February 1918, the county Board of Supervisors passed an ordinance to consolidate the township courts, which were now considered an "unnecessary expense to the taxpayers of the county." Judicial townships decreased from 26 to only five, obviously cutting the same number of judges and constables. The existence of this court was a tremendous convenience for the City of East San Diego, not to mention the source of a free and additional law enforcement officer for the area. It was probably with great disappointment that, on December 31, 1918, both Murray and Schilling were "mustered out of County service," as "both offices will automatically abolish with the coming of the new year." The two men were ESD residents and had served their respective offices (Schilling as Justice of the Peace and Murray as Town Constable) since 1914.

Murray became the branch manager at something called Irwin and Company, probably a real estate office, as that's the occupation listed for Murray in the 1921 San Diego City and County Directory. In July 1921, Murray was appointed night watchman by then City Marshal Bill Gray, after Officer Pat Shannon resigned that position. After only three months, Murray was "awarded" the managership of the Vista Theater, located at University and Copeland (42nd) Avenues.

Murray died of a heart attack in 1965 at age 80, in his East San Diego home on 46th Street. His obituary indicated he had worked as a sheriff's deputy and retired from that after 20 years. Murray had been a San Diego resident for 52 years and was survived by his wife, Mae, a son and two grandsons.

The First Term of James P. Ayers

James Payton Ayers: May 1914 to April 1915
Born: November 5, 1872 (Mississippi)
Died: September 27, 1944 (San Diego, California)

James P. Ayers was unique in the history of East San Diego law enforcement—he served as City Marshal twice. In April 1914, the City of East San Diego held municipal elections and a new administration was voted into office. The Trustees then entertained applications for the important marshal's post. Among the six or so candidates were George DeBarrow (a deputy marshal for Hyatt), C. E. Murray (former City Treasurer and future constable for the local Justice of the Peace), and Edward B. Hare (a future deputy marshal under William Gray). Curiously, the Board chose no one from that initial list. Instead, it voted on two longtime (for ESD) city residents: Nathaniel J. McHorney, Jr. and James P. Ayers.

McHorney belonged to an architectural firm and was secretary of the Young Republicans Club. His father was also well known in the community and a former lawman himself. Trustee and Police Commissioner Ira Markwith recommended McHorney for the top cop job. Ayers was a local real estate man nominated by the other trustee/police commissioner, Macpherson. The Board of Trustees voted 4-1 against McHorney and 3-2 for Ayers. J.P. Ayers was appointed the new city marshal on May 11, 1914. He was 41 years of age. His salary was set at $25 per month.

Ayers was born in Mississippi. His wife Lillian was also born there, where they presumably met and married. By 1900, they had a four-month-old daughter, Bulah, and were living in Calaveras, California. Ayers' occupation then was a barber. They had moved to Texas by 1909, where Lillian gave birth to her second daughter, Ruth. In Santa Anna, Texas, Ayers started his real estate career.

The Ayers family was living in the unincorporated community of City Heights when the area began its discussions of cityhood. Based on Ayers' municipal involvement, it is likely he was part of that process. As City Heights was established in a land boom, it made sense that a "real estater" would land there. By 1913, Ayers managed the Star Realty branch in ESD. Both the 1916 and 1917 city directories list Ayers with the "Holum & Ayers Realty Company."

Ayers was sworn into office on June 1, 1914. The 1914 City Directory listed "Jas P. Ayers" as both city marshal and tax collector. Wife Lillian served as third chairwoman for the local Woman's Assembly. Ayers quickly declared war on speeders (a chronic problem throughout the city's brief history) and dog "poisoners." The *East San Diego Press* added to the marshal's priorities, calling upon law enforcement to stop the local vandalism.

The first 10 months of Ayers' term seemed to go smoothly enough. A highlight was a visit from the governor of California. The grand home of R.O. Stensrud played host to Hiram Johnson (1911-1917) in the fall of 1914. This was a prestigious event that lent an element of class to the new city, to say nothing of more bragging rights.

The challenge of keeping a "dry" town led to a nasty spat between the city marshal and the board of trustees.

On March 28, 1915, Marshal Ayers appeared before the Board and requested the city not renew the license for poolroom operator Joseph E. Lynch. The marshal asserted Lynch was operating a "Blind Pig" at his 4014 Pauly (43rd) Avenue business — a Blind Pig being an establishment that illegally provided alcoholic beverages to its customers.[1] Although Ayers "failed to show where he had one bit of evidence," he openly made the charge after the board had renewed the license of three poolrooms. Ayers explained that he and "Gum-Shoe Sleuth" J.R. Davis (who would later identify himself as a deputy city marshal) went on a spying expedition and saw a man in the business "who seemed to be drunk." That man had a jug in his possession.

Trustee Markwith asked if Ayers had any evidence, to which Ayers replied he did not, though he had seen drunken men at the poolroom on several occasions. Markwith responded, "Why don't you do your duty like any police official and pinch the place?" Ayers indicated he required a search warrant for further investigation. Trustee Pfalher jumped in and suggested, "If you have any evidence do your duty and get one."

The Board decided to rescind the license and set a date for which Lynch was to show cause why his license

[1] The name originated in the 1800's, when so-called "blue" laws restricted the sale of alcoholic beverages. A saloonkeeper would charge customers to see an attraction (such as an animal) and provide a "complimentary" alcoholic beverage, this circumventing the laws.

Credit: San Diego Historical Society

At left, the front entrance of the East San Diego State and Commercial Savings Bank on the southwest corner of University and Fairmount Avenues. It was here, on June 6, 1919, that two gunmen committed the first-ever bank robbery in the San Diego region.

should not be revoked. This did not save Ayers from the wrath of newspaper editors who charged that, on more that one occasion, Ayers made arrests without any convicting evidence. The *Press* also asserted that, in all such cases, the city recorder had discharged the "victims" of Ayers' inefficient police ability.

In the same issue, editors chided that, "City Marshal J.P. Ayers really, sometimes, had evidence enough to convict, when makin [sic] an arrest."

The following week, Lynch lost his pool hall license. He admitted the presence of liquor, but claimed it was for his own personal use. In the fallout, the city also lost its marshal. Ayers resigned over the poolroom incident.

6

Marshal Austin Cole Steps In

Austin Robert Cole, Jr.: April 9, 1915 to April 17, 1916
Born: February 1, 1888 (New York)
Died: May 10, 1935 (San Diego, California)

Austin Cole was appointed on April 9, 1915, just 27 years of age. Born in New York and a plumber by trade, he was serving ESD as its city plumbing inspector when he took on his new task. The 1910 US Census listed Cole as a resident of City Heights with his wife Daisy E. and their 11-month-old son, Donald Edward Cole. However, the local City Directory never listed his family. When Cole registered for the draft in 1917, he listed himself as a widower with a seven-year-old son. By 1920, young Donald Cole was living with his widowed aunt, Fannie Cole Verity, in Los Angeles.

Though the reasons for his selection are unknown, Cole seemed a popular choice. After the apparent divisiveness of the previous marshal, the city was probably looking for someone to just do the job competently with little fanfare. Upon the announcement of his appointment, the large crowd attending the Trustee meeting responded with "a wild demonstration." It's hard to know whether Cole was that well liked or folks were just happy to be rid of Ayers. But Ayers would return.

Though he had no identifiable experience in law enforcement, Cole was forthwith in executing his duties. In May 1915, he arrested an 18-year-old for "committing a serious crime against an eight-year-old girl." Only months later, Cole found himself under fire as well, from a community that never seemed to be happy with its law enforcement. But the *East San Diego Press* took up his defense.

In "Just A Little Story About Our Marshal," the ESD shill chastised the "folks in the thriving little city...who delight in trying to run down and spread rumors." The unnamed writer practiced some early investigative reporting and noted there was no "evidence which tended to show that the marshal was not doing his duty." Instead, they discovered the marshal *was* doing his job. "Besides," the writer made point, "(Cole) is only paid the insufficient sum of $25 per month." The paper summarized that Cole had "proven himself to be the most efficient (police officer) the city ever had," and Cole's "friends are determined to down" any such vicious negative rumors.

That over, Cole continued his role as the top cop in town. In October 1915, a huge carnival came to ESD. Cole was authorized by City Trustees to hire 20 special policemen to preserve order the day of the event. The marshal immediately swore in the entire Carnival Committee and the local (volunteer) fire department. The grand day went off without a hitch.

The following month, Cole was instructed to employee a "night man." "The midnight prowlers who have been pilfering the milk bottles, robbing ice boxes of delicacies and stealing bread from back porches...had better be on their guard, for East San Diego has employed a night policeman." The city had grown to a point where law enforcement was required beyond the normal workday. The name of the new officer was not mentioned, though former City Marshal Frank A. Hyatt was later listed as a deputy marshal under Cole.

East San Diego continued to grow. In January 1916, exciting news about the University Avenue streetcar line extension to Euclid Avenue hit the papers, behind which David Ryan was a driving force.[1] As city elections neared, another force began to get its voice.

The East San Diego Civic League was formed to support specific candidates for various municipal offices. The goal was to determine endorsements for the nominations of the upcoming city election. When the Civic League met in February 1916, James P. Ayers served as its chairman. As the association only entertained support letters, William Gray objected and questioned the august body: Had his letter of endorsement been received? Apparently it was not, so Gray spoke on his own behalf. League members evidently were not impressed, as Gray did not carry an endorsement. A week later, Gray announced his candidacy for the Board of Trustees. Gray would lose this first effort, would try and lose again in two years, and have to settle for the City Marshal's position.

The local newspaper would soon take issue with the Civic League. A church-based organization (though apparently opposed by the "real church people of the city"), the League reportedly was formed by Southern Illinois

---

[1] Ryan later built the Silverado Tower and Ballroom in the early 1930's, and added to the Egyptian Garage; these structures still stand at Euclid and University Avenues.

lawyer F.G. "Boss" Blood. The *ESD Press* asserted Blood was a "petty politician of the old school," and had simply created a political ticket that pledged to appoint him to the office of City Attorney. Apparently, Blood felt that position would be a "pork barrel"[2] for him.

The Civic League was also poised to reappoint Ayers to his old job as City Marshal. Ayers was not a popular choice, reported the *ESD Press,* as he "was at one time city marshal but was asked to hand in his resignation by the present city officials for a mighty good reason."

On April 10, 1916, elections ushered in a new regime of city officials. A week later, Marshal Austin Cole tendered his resignation. The new Board of Trustees nominated Edward Hare and James Ayers for the top lawman job. Hare had been an earlier nominee for the position, back in 1914. He fared no better this time, as Ayers was named marshal by a three-to-two vote.

After his year as city marshal, Austin Cole settled back into what he seemed to know best—plumbing. Shortly after his resignation, Cole journeyed to Arizona, expecting "to be gone several months." The 1920 United States Census indicated Cole was residing in Globe, Arizona, but he was back in East San Diego the following year.

Cole did his civic duty in 1917, by registering for the draft, and was noted in the *East San Diego Press* "Roll of Honor" for having done so, along with scores of other ESD men. Cole was identified as a "former city marshal," one of the very few times his old law enforcement days would be mentioned.

---

[2] n. Slang: A government project or appropriation that yields jobs or other benefits to a specific locale and patronage opportunities to its political representative.

Credit: San Diego Historical Society

The East San Diego City Hall in 1919. The building was constructed in 1912 and housed a furniture store until it became available in April 1916. Then for the first time, city services and departments were consolidated into one location. Later and into the 1950's, the City Hall served as a substation for SDPD. The building remains in use today, though slightly altered, as a series of storefront businesses.

Cole was still living in the community of East San Diego when the exposition came to town in 1935. Cole hired on as a plumber. On May 10, 1935, he climbed under the Palace of Foods and Beverages to do some work. Assistant D.H. Hosea became concerned when Cole did not return, so Hosea went to see what happened. He found the plumber unconscious. Cole was taken to a first aid station, where he was pronounced dead. He was just 47 years of age. An autopsy was to have been conducted. His death was said to have been the first since the building of the Exposition had begun.

Austin Cole was buried with his parents at Greenwood Cemetery.

The Tumultuous Return
of Marshal Ayers

Second term: April 1916 to May 1918

Though the *East San Diego Press* noted Ayers "served as city marshal under the former administration but after having some trouble with the board he resigned," his second term began smoothly enough. Since the reckless operation of motor vehicles was a universal and perennial issue, Ayers "declared war on all automobile drivers."

The impetus for this declaration was the traffic death of "Little Orlen Fewett," who had been struck as he alighted from a stopped streetcar. By city ordinance, drivers were required to come to a dead stop 10 feet from a streetcar that was either collecting or discharging its passengers. The offender here failed to follow law and killed the boy on the street. Ayers sternly warned "that both rich and poor will be treated alike and that no excuse will be accepted" in the enforcement of this edict.

[1] "HOBSON & CLOUGH FURNITURE COMPANY, E O Hobson, F D Clough 5802 University av, ESD."

City Trustees delighted at the end of April, when the Toole Building became vacant and available. Originally a furniture store[1] and located on the northeastern corner of University and Van Dyke Avenues, the structure was large enough for the City to realize a small dream—to consolidate and house all City departments at one location. By June 1, 1916, the new City Hall was up and running. The building was now home to the President and City Trustees, the police and fire departments, tax assessor, and other city offices. This structure would serve the Cities of East San Diego and then San Diego until the 1950's. It survives today as a storefront for multiple businesses.

In July 1916, Ayers was called to investigate a suspicious occurrence on the streetcar line. Shortly after midnight on Friday the 14th, as the streetcar shifted at its terminus on University and Euclid Avenues, the trolley conductor had noticed some "supposed highwaymen" rise up from the sagebrush at Sierra Avenue (47th Street) and start in the direction of the car. The conductor signaled the motorman to go. "In this move the conductor claims that he avoided a hold-up." No suspects were ever apprehended.

Days later, Ayers and Constable C.E. Murray led a raid upon a "questionable house" located at 4422 Estrella Avenue. The headline suggested a previous incident ("Raided Again"), but failed to give further details. Four people (three women and one man) were caught in the house and brought before the City Recorder on vagrancy charges. Though the newspaper seemed loath to mention it, the intimation was prostitution activity. The reporter noted the notoriety of one arrestee, Flo Stewart, in connection with the infamous "Pink House" of

El Cajon Boulevard. While the suspects were released on bail and ordered to appear in court, the Pink House controversy would soon loom large in the City's eye.

Common thievery was another problem, one with which even the "Golden Rule" city had to contend. A September 1916 article warned that both City Marshal Ayers and Deputy Silas Puryear were on the lookout for the petty crooks targeting a myriad of small items: garden hoses and fruit. In one case, "prowlers" entered a house on Sisson (40th) Street and "carried away several bushels of figs." A few nights later and in the same neighborhood, a watermelon patch was "cleaned." Ayers urged residents to lock up their hoses at night. He believed most of the thievery was being done by boys and had several under suspicion.

At the end of August 1916, a court case erupted that had its roots in a controversy brewing in East San Diego since its inception. A former city trustee filed libel suit over words and opinions expressed in an unofficial ESD newsletter. The subject: Liquor.

East San Diego had established itself as a "dry" city at its incorporation. Trustees and law enforcement alike enforced these prohibition laws, as exemplified in the Bradt Street Raid of 1913. But by 1915, two camps seem to occupy each side of the liquor issue or—perhaps more accurately—different views of the same side.

One of the first conflicts came to light in April 1915, when Marshal Ayers asked the Board of Trustees to deny a business license on the grounds the operator was surreptitiously allowing liquor on the premises. Ayers was chastised for not doing his duty and, as a result, tendered his resignation. However, the board did not renew the business license.

Fast forward to January 1916: Voters turn down a proposal to allow "table liquor" at the Royal Japanese Tea Garden. This small flashpoint seemed to draw the lines between those who would tolerate limited, heavily licensed alcohol and those who would tolerate no allowance for liquor in this city. The concern that any liquor is too much liquor seems to have been the impetus for the formation of a new political committee.

Enter one Fred G. Blood, a lawyer from Illinois. He organizes the East San Diego Civic League, ostensibly a faith-based organization. A number of prominent ESD citizens join, including James Ayers, who served as chairmen. Initially, the League seemed to have been created for the purpose of endorsing nominees in the upcoming city election. But the *East San Diego Press* soon took the group to task with an imposing Page 1 article, " 'BOSS' BLOOD —HIS LEAGUE?"

"Politicians are of two kinds, there are big ones and little ones. The big ones, upon opportunity, become statesmen. The little ones never glimpse an opportunity beyond the field of narrow cunning, artifice, and intrigue."

Up to that point, the newspaper had made an effort to remain neutral on the liquor subject, especially in the January 1916 election, though it seemed to support the idea of limited liquor sale in its rant against the opposition's zealous argument. But the *Press* took exception to the League's broad attacks on the elected council. "The main idea of this church organization is to create the impression that every member of the present city administration is crooked, in order to foster personal ambition of the league leaders."

The *Press* accused (by way of the fact that it "has been freely reported about the city") the Civic League of endorsing candidates who had pledged to appoint Blood as city attorney and J.P. Ayers as city marshal.

The League published the "Saturday Telegram" to espouse its own thoughts and rhetoric on the subject. The opposing sides reached a crescendo with the city elections, when the voters had the final say. The result was basically a split decision, with an even number of winning candidates having been endorsed by the League. Their first duty after being sworn in was the immediate appointment of city department heads. Fred Blood won the job as City Attorney. James Ayers was reappointed as the City Marshal, the victor by 3-2 against the other nominee for the position, Edward Hare.

So the dust seemed to settle for the summer. The city went about its business, having seemingly moved past the fireworks of the most recent elections. But on the last day of August 1916, the most notorious civil suit in the short history of East San Diego opened in Judge C.N. Andrews' San Diego courtroom, rupturing old and not-yet-healed wounds within the city's political body.

Former ESD trustee W.N. Pfahler had filed a $50,000 libel suit, naming the Civic League, the Telegram Publishing Company, and 16 League members. Pfahler asserted that an article in the League's publication, the *Saturday Telegram,* was both malicious and libelous. The trial opened to a packed courtroom, with only one of the 12 jurors being from the Golden Rule City. Pfahler was the first witness called, testifying that the article in question had injured both his reputation and business.

Credit: San Diego Historical Society

Vehicular traffic is light on University Avenue in 1922. The Vista Theatre, a building that stands today as a grocery store, is seen at the southeastern corner of Copeland Street (now 42nd).

The daily *San Diego Union* had buried the trial story way back on Page 14, but to the weekly *East San Diego Press* it was front-page news. In fact, most its front page and much of three others detailed the convoluted, tedious story. Reading like a court transcript, the *Press* article went on *ad naseum*, though understandably so. This was big news in the little city.

Among the numerous witnesses called to the stand was Constable C.E. Murray, who spoke to matters regarding the infamous Pink House. Future marshal William Gray added that he wanted to raid that Pink House on several occasions, but was told each time that such a raid would have to coincide with an election, suggesting a political aspect for maximum impact. City Marshal Ayers recounted the encounter in his previous term, when he opposed the license reapplication of a pool hall he felt was serving

The "Motor Patrolman" Squad of the San Diego Police Department in 1927. Former East San Diego Chief Nat McHorney was assigned to this squad and can be seen standing fourth from left.

liquor. What came to light here was that, while trustees followed Ayers' advice on the pool hall, he was still asked to resign. Even Ayers' wife, Lillian, was called to speak of the internal meeting workings of the Civic League.

After about a week, the case went to the jury. In the wee hours of Saturday, September 9, 1916, the jury was deadlocked, so Judge Andrews locked them up for the night. This action seemed to motivate the jury. A verdict came later that day.

The jury found for the defendants, refusing to grant any damages to W.N. Pfahler. As a consolation, jurors officially commended the former trustee and his "associates for their efforts to maintain good government in East San Diego."

The *ESD Press* was not all too concerned about winners or losers; they wanted to see the peace kept in their fair city. Editors posted a Page 1 article that did not even report the outcome of the case, but instead asked for "a burial of past grievances and a new spirit of co-operation (sic), helpfulness and community pride."

With that little spectacle over, East San Diego seemed to get on with life. And Marshal Ayers was back on the job.

Days after the libel judgment, Ayers was following up on a burglary from the Harrington Grocery store at University and Highland Avenues. The criminals took cash and some sodas. The marshal suspected these to be the same boys who had recently taken Al Olson's car from 4038 Van Dyke Avenue on the same evening (Wednesday, September 13, 1916). Those may have been the very same suspects who had been annoying the town with a recent rash of petty thefts (garden hoses and fruit). Whether those under suspicion were ever brought to justice is not known, but Ayers was said to be hard at work gathering evidence in pursuit of an arrest.

A month later, Ayers apparently deputized city engineer Paul Ford after receiving a telephone call about trouble at Orange and Estrella Avenues. It was early on a Saturday morning and the Finnicum house was being "robbed." The suspect was GOA—gone on arrival—but the lawmen were determined to solve this crime, so they checked a nearby canyon and found Charles Griffin, age 60, with "a sack full of loot." Ford was credited with the arrest and booking of perpetrator.

All this crime (especially going on in the late night hours) led citizens to petition city trustees to employ a night watchman (no mention was made of the earlier move to do the same). Residents reasonably asked the City to pay part of the proposed officer's salary and some merchants agreed to contribute the other half. Inexplicably, Trustee Martin objected to any use of city money for a "night man." He could see no need, as he felt East San Diego was one of the most orderly communities in the country. Martin added that he understood a recent raise for the city marshal (to $85 a month) had been enacted to enable Ayers to pay part of a night watchman's salary. Though some impropriety

S.D. Police Historical Assn.

When the City of San Diego annexed East San Diego in 1923, the city also took over the ESD City Hall for municipal services. Because of its "remote location," SDPD established a sub station there as well, to better serve the newest citizens of San Diego. Posing in front of their station are officers assigned to Substation No. 3 (East San Diego) in 1927. On the far left is Motorcycle Officer Dean C. Benter.

was suggested, the matter was quickly referred to the police committee, who never reported back.

Coincidently, the *ESD Press* ran a self-promoting article in the very next issue, proclaiming "East San Diego Boasts No Jail." As if to remind themselves and their neighbors, the voice of the city proudly asserted they had no jail and needed no jail because they had little use for a jail. In fact, according to the paper, ESD had not a single arrest during its first 12 months of existence. The only idle men in town were the policemen. And, to throw in a minor non-sequitor, the original city trustees served entirely without pay (though that was no longer the case).

Motor Officer D.C. Benter, who joined SDPD in January 1921. He apparently was familiar with the territory, as the East San Diego Press *mentioned him chasing a speeder through the town in July 1921.*

For Marshal Ayers' next project, he took on gambling. Apparently acting on his own, Ayers banned the use of all slot machines and punchboards in town. City trustees quickly disagreed with Ayers' actions, as they delayed the action and told Ayers to allow the machines to be operated.

Reading between the lines, there seemed to be much disagreement between the trustees and marshal. While the media put a decidedly neutral (and often positive) spin on these incidents, it is clear that Marshal Ayers had a different view of law enforcement than his bosses. One party or another apparently learned to give—most probably the marshal—as Ayers was not removed after these squabbles, as was often the case in the city marshal

San Diego Police motorcycle officers in 1922. From left: B.W. Johnston, A.I. Comstock, M.C. Neely, and D.C. Benter. Johnston and Benter were noticed in the East San Diego Press *as passing through the city in pursuit of a speeding 19-year-old youth.*

system. Indeed, the year 1917 seemed a calmer one for both Ayers and the city at large.

Ayers chased and caught speeders (though it is unknown whether the city used any kind of marked police car), arrested unlicensed peddlers, and swooped down on an alleged disorderly house with his Deputy Silas Puryear, where seven "soldier boys" and an equal number of "girls" had emptied a number of liquor bottles. Puryear was guarding the rear door with a .45 Colt semi-automatic pistol as military police took their men away. The girls were reportedly set free.

With traffic a constant problem, city trustees purchased several "dummy policemen," or traffic stand signs, for University Avenue intersections at both Fairmount and Pauly (43rd) Avenues. Constable C.E. Murray joined Marshal Ayers in insisting the public recognize them as official traffic devices. The paper charged that "a great per cent of all the automobile accidents occurring in the city street as due to disregard for traffic laws."

In August 1917, the *ESD Press* ran a piece supporting Ayers' work as city marshal. Highlighting the period from April 18, 1916 (Ayers' second appointment) until May 1, 1917, the article listed statistics to support their good will. Ayers and his deputies averaged over 100 "complaints and calls" per month. Among the cases worked by the marshal:

- 3 burglaries
- 2 attempted burglaries
- 2 cases of "threatening to kill"
- 3 cases of wife beating
- 12 cases for drunkenness and disturbing the peace
- 10 women fined for vagrancy
- 20 cases of city and state traffic laws
- 95 other charges
- 34 known prostitutes left ESD during the first six months

Assistance was acknowledged from other law enforcement agencies, including the San Diego Police Department, the sheriff's office, and various federal offices. Special credit was extended to Constable C.E. Murray and the district attorney's office, especially in regard to the closing of the notorious "Pink House" of prostitution. Everyone seemed to be getting along just fine and, by the close of 1917, Marshal Ayers asserted he would be strictly enforcing the new state speed laws due to go into effect on the first of the New Year.

The New Year brought SDPD detectives Lopez and Sears to visit "this city," recovering nearly $1,500 worth of jewelry and clothing, stolen by a "gang" in San Diego.

On March 29, 1918, the newspaper triumphantly proclaimed, "Ayers Nabs Burglars." The "youthful" burglars, both 16 years of age, had victimized two local businesses: the Pfahler & Bayless Lunch Stand at Conklin (41St) and Anna (Polk) Streets on February 23rd and the Blanchard Grocery on March 16th. An unnamed fingerprint expert from the San Diego Police Department reportedly rendered some valuable assistance to Ayers, who elicited confessions from both of the juveniles. Interestingly, Pfahler was the former trustee who brought many townsfolk up on charges of libel, including one James Ayers.

The "political bees" were buzzing by February 1918, followed by the winds of change in April: "Present Marshal Ayers expecting his removal at any time." By May 10, Ayers was no longer the town's top cop, but he was still enforcing the law. The now "former" marshal made the papers when he "captured" two boys who had falsely activated a fire alarm box.

After a split term and three years, Ayers quit law enforcement for good. He returned to his old practice as a real estate broker—a popular occupation in those land-happy days of East San Diego. Ayers continued to live in East San Diego, even after the consolidation. He died there in 1944 at the age of nearly 72 years. His wife Lillian remained a resident until her death at age 82 in 1957.

Marshal Gray Heads
into the Modern Era

William H. Gray: May 3, 1918 to June 5, 1922
Born: February 1869 (Virginia)
Died: December 18, 1931 (San Diego, California)

With his four-year term, William H. Gray easily served the longest of any marshal for the City of East San Diego. His tenure would expand and diversify law enforcement in the little city. Now his organization would be called a "Police Department." Gray appointed night watchmen, traffic officers, and motorcycle cops to address the growing problems and concerns with a growing population.

As reported in February 1918 ("Political Bees Are Beginning To Buzz"), elections were only two weeks away and the *East San Diego Press* was throwing its support around. One of the potential candidates mentioned was "that Bill Gray—you know the guy—that fellow who can make as much noise as Roosevelt—but can't kick up as much dust ..." This would be Gray's second of three attempts to join the Board of Trustees. Though the paper did not

67

endorse Gray, they at least allowed him an advertisement. His platform was fairly simple: "Fearless Champion of the People's rights — Strong for Annexation."

From its very inception, whether to remain an incorporated city or join San Diego continued to be a hot topic in East San Diego. The arguments were varied but consistent on both sides. The *East San Diego Press* was an unabashed cheerleader for continued cityhood. In fact, the East San Diego Promotion Club advertised quite regularly in the newspaper, due in no small way to its president (George T. Ringe) and secretary (Roy O. Akers) being the editor and manager (respectively) of the publication.

Bill Gray carried some precincts, but was not elected as a Trustee. However, he almost immediately became a candidate for city marshal. Other applicants included the aforementioned Roy Akers and Edward Slinkard. Gray and Akers seemed the favored two and the *ESD Press* went to bat for its own. The paper reported that "the last few days had seen much opposition" to Gray, based on his actions to foster various annexation and disincorporation movements. The newspaper's support of its city was clear when it reported, "Most object to (Gray's) appointment under any circumstances." But in the week that followed, both Akers and Slinkard withdrew their applications. Headlines proclaimed the new appointee: William H. Gray, age 49, would be the next City Marshal.

Gray was born in Virginia in February 1869. He would meet and marry Annie L. Flippen and the two were in San Diego by 1900, where Gray worked as a finance agent. Together they had seven sons, all but one born in San Diego. Gray was living in City Heights when it incorporated.

Gray had quite a colorful history prior to becoming the fifth top cop of East San Diego. Apparently, he was a special investigator for Wells Fargo Express Company and worked as a guard during the St. Louis World Fair (1904).[1] He had reportedly "been in several Indian engagements" and was a Spanish-American War veteran, having commanded a company as a First Lieutenant in Cuba. He also served as a United States Marshal in Alameda County for four years.

By 1916, Gray was involved in ESD city politics. When the Civic League formed, Gray asked for an endorsement and was denied. He unsuccessfully ran for the Board of Trustees in March 1916. After that, he seemed to enjoy being a minor pain in the city's side. Addressing the Trustees in 1917, in an attempt to garner approval for the improvement of Auburn Drive (which had been damaged during the great floods of 1916), Gray was "jokingly" asked if he were against the government. Gray responded that while he was not against the United Stated government, but he *was* against the East San Diego government.

About a week after his appointment, Gray created his little department by deputizing a number of townsmen. These included such names as Al Olson (an auto theft victim in 1916), Ed Hare (an applicant for city marshal in 1914), Gus Nachant (a local businessman), Lester Davis, and Roy Akers (of the *ESD Press)*. He also appointed young "Buck" Hyatt[2], the City Engineer and son of the city's second marshal, Frank Hyatt. Gray was apparently the only

[1] Pliny Castanien, "Interview of Archer Gray," August 23, 1978.
[2] George Frank "Buck" Hyatt was the youngest of Frank Hyatt's four children. He later accepted the city engineer's position for Coronado, effective September 1, 1918. Buck later served as Coronado's City Manager.

paid member of the ESD-PD, with a salary of $50 a month. Later, Deputy Ed Hare would reportedly earn a $5 salary.

The newspaper gave account that the marshal was a "very busy man these days." His many and varied duties included "catching stray dogs, rendering assistance to suicide cases, (and) settling of neighborhood quarrels," as well as trying to catch the chronic dog poisoners (as stray animals seemed quite a problem for the city).[3]

Bill Gray wasted no time in the discharge of his duties. He was commended for finding a sick soldier lost in a canyon in the northeasterly part of the city. In June 1918, a house was "robbed" on Hugo Street (Central Avenue) and Gray was "on the trail." Police recovered footprint evidence from that scene.

August 1918 was a busy month for the ESD-PD. Marshal Gray captured two "boy burglars" who had escaped from reform school. The juveniles had "four or five guns" in their possession and several rounds of ammunition. Both confessed to their crimes. Another juvenile ("the youngest Kurtz boy") escaped from a detention camp and was captured by Gray. That suspect was able to get away from the marshal but was successfully chased down by Deputy Lester Davis, after several warning shots had been fired to (unsuccessfully) entice the lad into halting. Police also raided a "hop joint," where they confiscated numerous hypodermic needles, though no opium was found.

Gray's vigilance hit a bump in September 1918, when police raided a "Local Booze Center." Officers seized a "quantity of intoxicants" and arrested Mrs. Cathorina De Torrio from 3614 Van Dyke Avenue. Justice was swift in East San Diego as two weeks later the *Press* announced

[3] Stray dogs and cats seemed a chronic problem for East San Diego.

a hung jury. Mrs. De Torrio immediately filed a lawsuit against Marshal Gray and demanded $1,040 in damages. The Board of Trustees took up the lawsuit the very night it was filed, officially deciding "to back Gray to the limit." This backing was not unanimous, as Trustee Fitch took exception to the support. A week later, the case was again scheduled for court and again it ended in a hung jury.

Undeterred, Gray continued his local law enforcement. This time it was a case of infidelity, as the female suspect Troutman (the newspaper listed only the last name) was seeing another man while her husband was away in the service. A sailor was taken into custody at the Troutman home on Mission Street (Nile) and released to military police.

As 1918 came to a close, the world was hit with a deadly influenza pandemic. The insidious virus would claim 20 million people worldwide, 550,500 in the United States alone. Over 300 of some 70,000 persons living in the San Diego region died. The Health Board responded by issuing an official decree via the newspaper:

> "Be it resolved by the Board of Health of the City of East San Diego, that for the Public health and safety, which is threatened by an epidemic, the 'Spanish Fleu,' (sic) commencing immediately and continuing until further notice, all places of public gathering, such as churches, schools, public halls, place of amusement, etc, shall be closed."

Even a San Diego Police Department officer contracted the disease while on-duty and succumbed to it.[4] By early

---

[4] Officer Walter Holcomb is listed on the San Diego Police Department's Honor Roll of officers killed in the line of duty.

November, the contagion waned and the quarantine was called off.

But a month later, the worse that could happen did —the flu was back in full force. The East San Diego Health Board officially put the "Quarantine Lid On Again." An ordinance was quickly passed and masks were issued to residents. The area of particular concern was the center of town, an area bounded by Anna Street (Polk Avenue), Klauber Street (Wightman Avenue), Sisson Avenue (40th Street) and Highland Avenue, presumably the most densely populated part of the community. Gray and the East San Diego PD were called upon to enforce the so-called Mask Law.

Deputy Marshal Edward Hare reportedly contracted the incessant flu. Hare did finally recover, though it took two weeks to do so. At Christmastime, Gray received written notice that he could cease such enforcement, as the epidemic had finally run its course.

The New Year of 1919 brought more legal grief for Gray. One Pasqual Bernardeni filed suit against Gray, who was alleged to have held the man at gunpoint while deputies explored the Bernardeni premises pursuant to a search warrant. The plaintiff argued the September 1918 incident and the officers' presence directly caused the death of his wife the following October (the woman contracted influenza that led to pneumonia). Amazingly, Judge Andrews awarded the sum of $2,500 to Mr. Bernardeni. Gray asked for a retrial. Disincorporation groups latched onto the case like vultures on carrion, claiming the City of East San Diego would not be responsible for the fine if annexed by San Diego. The compensation was later cut to $250.

Gray then fell ill and was confined to his home for much of a week. This could have been leftover flu and/or stress

An SDPD officer poses in his green "olive drab" uniform, in front of a police ambulance parked next to the East San Diego City Hall. Circa 1928, the ESD City Hall served the community for many years following the dissolving of the city. Community pride and independence would remain strong for decades thereafter.

from the trial. Fortunately, the next few months leveled out. Though East San Diego was growing (6,000 in 1918, per the City Directory), there seemed to be no special crime problems, other than the usual juveniles and some vandalism. A major concern was speeding, as the automobile's use and popularity increased. That ESD-PD seemed to have no police cars in which to catch the speeders may have greatly contributed to a lack of enforcement.

As part of the constant effort to control speeders, Gray initiated a "crusade" on "fast automobile drivers." He enlisted the aid of the *San Diego Union* newspaper and was obliged with a front-page article. Gray boasted of 300 "arrests" (probably citations) in a five-week period, with 125 having been fined, and all for speeds of over 30 miles per

Credit: San Diego Historical Society

An "auto trap" in the 1920s, possibly the same one Marshal William Gray described in the May 13, 1919 edition of the San Diego Union. The men and location are not identified, but the man on the left could very well be Arthur Tocque, who was identified as "timing speeders" and receiving pay for such in the Council Minutes printed in the East San Diego Press *of December 21, 1920.*

hour. The motive for the increased enforcement: numerous complaints registered by ESD residents.

"The marshal carefully explained his system of catching speeders and said he had four men with stop watches along the road who timed every auto and if the machine was traveling over a certain number of seconds for the marked distance, the speed officers were given the signal and that auto driver would be arrested." No comment was made as to the method of the stop.

Archer Gray would later comment that "auto speeders" was his father's main enforcement problem, and that

Credit: San Diego Historical Society

The Bank of East San Diego opened on the northwest corner of University and Van Dyke Avenues in August 1923. Ironically, the city would fold by the end of that year. The building was restored in 2004 and is currently a neighborhood pub.

he did not have a car, so enforcement was problematic. This seemed to be the reason he hired Howard Jack, who would enforce traffic laws on his motorcycle.

Gray's interest and concern with traffic issues would result in a singular irony later in his career.

The apparent lack of a police car led to the need to be resourceful. When a report came in of a suspicious man carrying two suitcases in the area of the Chollas Navy Towers, Gray had no way to respond in a timely manner. So he hired a car, part of a regular "stage" line between San Diego and La Mesa, to get a ride to the eastern edge of ESD. There he found an undocumented person transporting prohibited alcohol and took the offender into custody.

On June 6, 1919, the city gained a dubious distinction—the site of the first-ever bank robbery in the county. This time, it was first page news in the *San Diego Union:*

BANK ROBBERS GET $5,000, FLEE FROM EAST
SAN DIEGO IN AUTOS

"In the first real bank robbery in this particular section of the United States…" began the article, with a
subtle glee. The big-city newspaper couldn't help but
sensationalize the embarrassing event, to the misery of
its little sister town.

The target had been the East San Diego Commercial and Savings Bank, on the southwestern corner of
University and Fairmount Avenues. At 2:50 PM, two
suspects entered the bank. They wore linen dusters and
"automobile" goggles and commanded that all the customers line up against the wall. One robber approached
a teller, pointed a "wicked looking" .45 caliber revolver,
and said, "Hands up —damn you." The robbers took
about 15 minutes to relieve the bank of nearly $11,000.[5]
Eight customers were also robbed at gunpoint, one being
Roy Akers. Their losses included several watches "and
a small but good assortment of stickpins." The robbers
fled east in a fast car.

Possibly because of the enormity of the event, both the
Sheriff's Department and the San Diego Police Department responded to the scene. After interviewing witnesses, police felt these suspects were not amateurs.

With the exception of a "Deputy Marshal Schlink[6] of
East San Diego," the city's police force was conspicu-
ously missing from the *San Diego Union's* coverage (The
East San Diego Press most likely covered the biggest event

[5] The initial estimate was about $5,000, but the next day a more accurate count
indicated the loss was $10,900.
[6] Possibly Deputy Marshal Edward Slinkard. Charles L. Schlink lived in San
Diego in 1912, but it is unknown if he ever served as a deputy marshal.

The San Diego Union *reports the first bank robbery in the history of San Diego County. Though the headlines reported a $5000 loss, the actual amount was closer to $11,000.*

of the young city's history, but no copies of that issue are known to exist). Undersheriff Ed Cooper directed sheriff's deputies (Sheriff Byers was out-of-town) and the SDPD was taking "much interest" in the case, with Detective Kelly handling the case for police. In fact, "police were combing the city" and had "questioned a number of persons whose reputation were not of the best." Though no one was held, the paper speculated that a possible roundup of bad characters by police was in order.

Marshal Gray may, in fact, have been a part of the hubbub. In a 1978 interview, Archer Gray relayed a story about his father and one of the biggest crimes to hit East San Diego: a bank robbery. Per his son, Marshal Gray was standing directly across the street from the bank when the robbery went down. The suspects got into a big, fast car and fled the scene. Gray could do little more than watch, as no car was available for pursuit.

If Marshal Gray had indeed witnessed the first bank robbery of the county, then the *San Diego Union* either was unaware or indifferent. Days later, the paper reported that bank employees had identified two suspects who were picked up in Ocean Beach. SDPD Detective (and future Chief) George Sears undertook the interrogation and quickly discovered a strange fact—the suspects knew personally his brother, who lived in Calexico, California. These two suspects were quickly exonerated and released.

Research has yet to reveal if the actual suspects in this crime were ever identified or apprehended.

Though Marshal Gray was tough on traffic violators, that recurring problem would catch up to him in a near fatal manner.

On December 8, 1920, shortly before 6 PM on a misty Wednesday evening, Bill Gray stepped from the south curb of University Avenue to cross Pauly (43rd) Street. He was suddenly struck by a vehicle and seriously injured. According to Myrle Morrison, the driver of the offending vehicle, a light mist was falling as he turned south from University Avenue onto Pauly. Morris said his headlights became dim as he made the turn, "as is the case with the Ford lights," and he "hit someone or something and stopped the car at once and found that it was the Marshal." Gray suffered a fractured skull and a badly bruised right arm and hand. A doctor was summoned to the scene and Gray was eventually taken to St. Joseph's Hospital in San Diego.[7]

The President of the Board of Trustees immediately appointed William L. Martin as the Acting Marshal while Gray convalesced at the hospital. Martin was a motorcycle officer who apparently continued in that assignment while filling in as city marshal.

[7] Located at 6th Street and University Avenue, was renamed Mercy Hospital in November 1924.

The following week's report indicated Gray was improving slowly and by the following month the marshal was walking with the aid of a cane. Though the reporter felt it would be some time before Gray would be able to return to work, it appears he was back and before the Board of Trustees by March 1921. Interestingly, Gray was calling attention to a couple of steel cages at the county jail that could be obtained and used by the city. This suggestion of a jail for the Golden Rule City did not result in the type of response as it did some years prior, in 1916, when Constable C.E. Murray suggested such idea. Maybe East San Diego had matured a little by then.

A full year after Gray's accident, he filed a $50,000 lawsuit against Morrison and his employers, Florenten and Hutchinson. Gray would later file a related suit against ESD. According to his son, Bill Gray was unable to work steady after that injury.

Though no formal announcement has been located, Gray must have taken it upon himself to address the traffic problems in a new and more effective manner. Perhaps the city was also ready financially. Whatever the case, traffic violators had a new nemesis to content with under Gray's administration—the motorcycle cop.

Council minutes printed in the *East San Diego Press* indicated three motorcycle officers working regularly for the PD: the aforementioned William L. Martin, Howard Fraser, and Howard W. Jack. Transcripts listed expense demands ranging as low as $16 to as much as $150. Most likely, these gentlemen supplied their own motorcycle, a routine procedure of the day. While it is not known whether these motor cops pulled a regular salary, presumably, these added expenses related to gasoline and other wear and tear of their job. The officers probably wore uniforms and worked daytime hours, but these facts cannot be confirmed. Certainly, the fines from their activity were substantial and a bonus to city coffers.

Early in 1921, the subject of a night watchman was again brought before council. President Sauer, chairmen of the Police Committee, recommended a police officer be appointed for night duty, with a salary of $90 a month, to commence on February 1, 1921. Further, he felt the city's purchasing agent should be instructed to purchase a bicycle for the night watchman's use. This equipment would be left at City Hall during the day, for use by other officers. The matter was apparently tabled, brought forth again at the February 1 meeting, and tabled a second time. Finally, with Sauer's recommendation that Marshal Gray submit three names for the position, the motion passed. Gray was ordered to have those candidates ready for the next trustee meeting.

Mr. Patrick Shannon was soon appointed the night watchman with unanimous approval.

Pat Shannon quickly proved his worth by arresting a young man who had attempted to rob John Bryant's grocery store, with an assist from Patrolman C. Jay Matthews. Marshal Gray was back at it in June, arresting a man for "drunkness" on Euclid Avenue and confiscating a bottle of wine from the car. Officer Matthews then assisted Marshal Gray in taking George McFadden into custody for "passing bad checks." Matthews kept busy with another arrest, being aided by a citizen in the arrest of Emil Rivers. Rivers made the unfortunate decision to drive while intoxicated, bringing attention to himself when he mowed down a row of mailboxes.

With Independence Day in the offing, Gray used the *East San Diego Press* to issue a safety admonition. He warned that guns, pistols, and fireworks were "a menace to life and property" and were "absolutely taboo" for the upcoming 4th of July 1921 celebration.

C.E. Murray became the new night watchman in July 1921. Affectionately nicknamed "Bunny," Murray had served as township constable for the Mission district in ESD, before that office was consolidated and phased out by the County Board of Supervisors. He seemed quite a character, once advocating that killing the city's worthless dogs and cats would somehow help the government win the war (that would be World War I). A chicken fancier, Murray was also a founder of the Progress and Prosperity Club. He took over for Pat Shannon, who had resigned on June 30. Murray relinquished the assignment three months later, in favor of the Vista Theater "managership." Nat McHorney quickly filled the opening left by Murray.

In early 1922, Gray made a third unsuccessful attempt to get elected to the Board of Trustees. Though he again carried a couple of precincts, he again lost his bid. The *East San Diego Press* printed his gracious "thank you" letter he wrote to those who had supported his run for office.

In May 1922, Gray requested and was granted two weeks leave of absence, with intent to visit Los Angeles. Maybe he saw the writing on the wall, for he had lost his job less than a month later. The former marshal later sued the city, claiming he had been incapacitated while on duty and that he was a "dutiful and worthy officer" who had been discharged without cause, "other than (for) political reasons."

In 1928, Gray ran for the county sheriff's office, but lost to Byers. Gray died at his home at 3505 49th Street in East San Diego on December 18, 1931, after having been in failing health for sometime. He was 63.

The Last Marshal:
Nat McHorney

Nathaniel Joseph McHorney, Jr.: June 5, 1922 to December 1923
Born: May 16, 1885 (Jersey City, New Jersey)
Died: June 5, 1956 (San Diego, California)

On June 5, 1922, 37-year-old Nat McHorney was appointed the new and last marshal of East San Diego. Though he probably had no idea, McHorney would guide the ESD-PD to its ultimate demise and incorporation into the San Diego Police Department on December 23, 1923.

Nathaniel J. McHorney Jr. was born in Jersey City, New Jersey on May 16, 1885. His mother died early in his life, as by age 15 "Nat" was living with his father and his aunt. The McHorneys had arrived in City Heights by 1910. Papa Nat lived with his 2nd wife, Anna, having started another family (with kids aged one to three and more to come). He was serving as a county sheriff's deputy at that time.

Nat Jr. married a native of Mexico (Charlotte) and the two would have seven children together. McHorney worked for the Spreckels Company and the local Electric

Railway Company when East San Diego was voted into existence. He served as secretary of the Young Republican's Club of East San Diego and was an early candidate for the city marshal's position in 1914, but lost that appointment to James Ayers. McHorney was the city's night watchman for eight months leading into his appointment as the top cop.

McHorney immediately called for all former deputy city marshals to turn in their badges (by way of an article in the *ESD Press)*, so that he could officially appoint his own deputies. Apparently, the cost of new badges was prohibitive. Among those he deputized were Howard Jack (originally hired by Gray), P.G. Kerr, Jr., and Edward Joseph Moore, Jr. He and Moore apparently were good friends, as both were natives of New Jersey. In fact, Moore and his family would later attend the McHorney's grand 18th wedding anniversary.

The new marshal then began to address lawbreakers. McHorney put dog owners on notice by warning them to either pay to license their pets or a warrant for their arrest would be issued for the violation. He warned bicyclists to stay clear of the sidewalks, as that was also a violation of city ordinance. Then he and Deputy Marshal Howard Jack made a discovery for the local history books.

The headlines were bold: "Largest Still In History Of San Diego County Found By Nat McHorney." McHorney and Jack had eyes on some unusual traffic over on Thomas (38th) Street. The two lawmen "worked on the case for two weeks," believing the house might be a "hop headquarters" — an opium den—as many Chinese were seen to frequent the place. On Monday, June 26, McHorney and Jack raided the residence of E.R. Henrickson,

Credit: San Diego Historical Society

At right, the Fairmount Apartments survive today on the southwestern corner of University Avenue and 43rd Street. In December 1920, City Marshal William Gray stepped from this curb at dusk and was hit by a car. He suffered moderate injuries and was able to return to work several months later.

accompanied by a "Prohibition Officer," a U.S. narcotics agent, and detectives from both San Diego Police and the sheriff's office. They captured Henrickson as he was leaving "in a machine" (i.e., an automobile). Inside the house they found a small amount of opium. A search of the backyard revealed a small structure disguised as a chicken coop. Inside, officers found a huge 50-gallon still, along with 17 gallons of moonshine whiskey and about 750 gallons of corn mash. The whiskey was confiscated and the corn mash poured down the canyon.

Sometime later, McHorney outdid himself with another booze arrest, this time locating a 60-gallon copper still at 3396 33rd Street.

Credit: San Diego Historical Society

On the south side of the 4200 block of University Avenue, the business district was full of activity in the early 1920s. Billiard parlors were popular entertainment centers of the era.

Ever vigilant, McHorney made the papers again for capturing an escapee from a Los Angeles chain gang and jailing an auto theft suspect.

By all accounts, the East San Diego Police Department was running efficiently under McHorney. But the city was under assault from the "disincorporatinists" once again. Though the city had successfully defended itself on numerous prior occasions, a series of events would simultaneously create the opening for which to end the City of East San Diego.

When the end finally came, McHorney segued smoothly into the San Diego Police Department. Officially appointed on February 12, 1924, he was initially assigned to his old neighborhood, the new East San Diego police sub station. There he worked as a "motor patrolman." He continued as an effective and active lawman, his work often noted in the local press. One of the more interesting calls occurred in August 1925.

A passerby had called police to report a flaming cross burning in the front yard of 4058 Pauly (43rd) Street, the home of now 80-year-old Frank Hyatt, former ESD city marshal. Four unidentified men had planted the KKK symbol there, then threw a rock at Hyatt's front door and "beat a hurried retreat." Hyatt reportedly sat calmly inside his home during the ruckus, reading a newspaper. Patrolman McHorney responded to the call and tore down the cross, and then went inside to find Hyatt still reading his paper. Hyatt merely laughed at the incident. Neighbors told McHorney that Hyatt was opposed to the racist organization and had been recently voicing that opinion. The result was some ill feelings that had been previously expressed with a number of notes signed "KKK" and bearing the "skull and crossbones" mark. These notes warned Hyatt to leave the city or someone might "get" him. Hyatt's response? He was ready to be "got" at any time.

McHorney seemed to have a knack for being in the right place at the right time. In 1930, he was vacationing in the Cuyamaca Mountains when a seven-year-old came up missing. McHorney led a search for a lost boy, who was found after 28 hours in the wilderness, safe and sound. In fact, it was McHorney's party who located the boy.

Three years later, McHorney headed another search for a missing boy, this time in Balboa Park. This ending was not so happy—the boy's body was found in the bay six days after he went missing. He had been murdered, possibly part of an unsolved serial killer series.

S.D. Police Historical Assn.

The last City Marshal of East San Diego, Nat McHorney poses at his desk. He went on to a successful career as a homicide detective for the San Diego Police Department.

McHorney took a promotional exam in 1928 and passed. Chief George Sears eventually promoted him to detective in 1934. His many assignments included the police forgery detail the robbery unit, and property crimes. McHorney finally landed in the Homicide Unit, where he remained until his retirement on August 2, 1940.

The last city marshal lived out his life in his old community. At age 71, McHorney died in his East San Diego resident at 4172 Wightman Street in June 1956. His wife Charlotte, four daughters, three sons, two brothers, six sisters, and 16 grandchildren survived him.

The City of San Diego
Takes Over

By 1923, East San Diego's population had grown to 12,000. From its very incorporation, East San Diego had a nearly equally sized faction that was adamant the city should not be a city. Over its 11-year history, this faction brought plans for disincorporation to a public vote on numerous occasions. After frequent embarrassments and controversies, it was a finally a severe water shortage that may have been the final nail in the city's coffin.

On June 26, 1923, ESD citizens went to the polls to again decide the issue of annexation. At the end of the day, 1,344 voters overruled 1,109 to consolidate with its larger, older neighbor (and namesake), the City of San Diego.

San Diego elected officials determined they needed an election of their own; as such an annexation would have financial consequences. Though this gave the proponents of East San Diego some temporary hope, San Diego voters approved the municipal appropriation in October 1923.

The City of East San Diego officially "passed into history" at noon on December 23, 1923. San Diego's city council and department heads traveled to the ESD City Hall to participate in a "ceremony of consolidation," formally taking over records and installing deputies to various positions. San Diego Police Chief James A. Patrick appointed Nat McHorney, Jr. "and others of the former East San Diego police and traffic force" to his Department, with orders to temporarily proceed with their work in the newest suburb of San Diego. Patrick then issued municipal badges to all the old ESD officers.

Not all former ESD organizations adapted so well. The volunteer fire department refused to disband until June 1924. The former ESD police officers mostly made a smooth transition. As mentioned earlier, McHorney had discovered his calling, becoming a top homicide detective in the 1930's and until his retirement in 1940.

Howard Jack became an SDPD motorcycle officer, a duty he had performed for ESD-PD. He too often worked the East San Diego area. On one occasion, Jack came across a stolen car full of juvenile boys. He determined the car had only been "borrowed" for their fun and the boys were actually in the act of returning it when Jack took them into custody. Interesting to note was the fact that two of the boys—Albert Gray and Gene McHorney—were the sons of the two city marshals he formerly worked under in ESD.

Jack had a good run as an SDPD officer, finally retiring in 1944. Edward Moore's epilog is more tragic.

Moore was 22 years old when ESD ceased to exist. San Diego PD immediately picked him up, but they soon realized he was too young for the job. SDPD hiring standards required a minimum age of 25 —Moore was still three years shy of that birthday. So he was "relieved from duty (not on eligible list)" on August 31, 1924. He rejoined the

December 30, 1923: Headlines herald the merger and a tale of two cities: East San Diego becomes, simply, San Diego.

department on October 1, 1929. His career would be cut tragically short just three years later.

On January 7, 1933, Moore had just completed his work shift on a Saturday night. He left police headquarters (then on 500 2nd Street), driving his personal car and still in uniform, en route his East San Diego residence (4293 47th Street). As Moore passed 13th and "G" Streets, he saw a man acting suspiciously. Moore realized the man fit the description of an armed robber described earlier in the day. Compelled to do his duty, Moore stopped to question the suspect.

There he contacted Eddie Arbello (who also went by Harry Smith). Moore conducted a pat down for his own safety and discovered a .32 caliber in the man's waistband. Moore recovered the gun and stuck it in his own waistline. His police instincts confirmed, Moore decided to transport Arbello back to HQ. He was in the process of placing the man into his personal car when Arbello lashed out.

Arbello punched Moore in the face, then grabbed the gun from the cop's waistline and fired twice. Moore was hit in the chest, one round passing through the 1933 Vehicle Code in his breast pocket. Moore collapsed to the sidewalk and Arbello shot him again. Despite a bullet

Credit: San Diego Historical Society

December 1923: A crowd gathers as old city limits fade away, University and Boundary Avenues. Plans called for the word "East" to be replaced with the word "Greater," something that never came to pass.

through the lung, Moore managed to get up and chase Arbello, who fled the crime scene. Moore fired several rounds at the fleeing suspect and again collapsed.

Officers responded en masse. In fact, a motorcycle officer was seriously injured when he rear-ended a detective car also en route the scene. Arbello had secreted himself under a house at 728 14th Street. Among the officers to locate and take Arbello into custody was Nat McHorney, Moore's old boss and friend from their East San Diego days.

When questioned, Arbello could only say that he just went crazy and had no reason for attacking Officer Moore.

Eddie Moore's prognosis was 50-50 when he first reached the hospital. However, days later he developed pneumonia. He succumbed to injuries and illness on

January 15, 1933, just 33 years of age. He left behind his wife, Sophia, and two children, one an 18-month old. Arbello was convicted of murder and sentenced to a life in prison.

The East San Diego community remained fiercely independent for decades. The "East San Diego" sign hung over the intersection of University and Fairmount Avenues into the 1970's. But as the community aged and property values crashed, another sort of land boom began. The idea was to create a new customer base to turn around the flagging and fleeing business community. The easy answer was to increase the number of residents and the easiest way to do that was to build more residences. In 1965, the San Diego City Council approved the new Mid-City Community Plan.

Then the developers went to work. House upon home was purchased for next-to-nothing and razed, to be replaced by apartment buildings. Some of these complexes were huge, taking up the site of a dozen or more former single-detached dwellings. The owner population was quickly replaced with a renter group and middle-class residents began to flee in large numbers. Community pride withered as the new transient population grew. Crime rose sharply as gangs and drug dealers took advantage of the area. Violence increased and became commonplace.

In 1971, the San Diego Police Department opened a community relation's storefront at 40th Street and University Avenue to create Neighborhood Watch programs. This effort to reduce crime, or at least deflect it, was only marginally successful, as crime continued to rise.

As the community population grew from some 45,100 in 1980 to over 67,500 in 1990, any quality of life began

Credit: San Diego Historical Society

Erected in 1952, the "East San Diego" community sign hung proudly over the intersection of University and Fairmount Avenues until it was removed in 1969, to widen the streets. If there were any plans to replace it, they never came to fruition. But fiery independence of the community seemed to fade with the memory of this symbol.

to vanish for the still viable but neglected residents. Suddenly, no one seemed to care for this community and many even feared it.

The name "East San Diego" fell out of favor, as it now represented a crime-ridden community.

The 1980's saw a tremendous influx of refugees, mostly from Southeast Asia. Vacant storefronts began to fill with new and diverse businesses. A new community voice began to rise, mixed in part with old residents who never gave up and new folks who now called the area their home.

As the rebirth continued, the community began to redefine itself for the future and so reached back for a name from the past. Though the moniker never really went away, the new voice called for the name of City Heights to represent the opportunity and hope of the resurrected community.

The engineers of change quickly realized the overriding necessity for a regularly staffed police station, where citizens and law enforcement could come together to apply the new "Neighborhood Policing" model being practiced by the San Diego Police Department. The idea of a "Mid-City" facility had been bandied around since the 1980's, but time and money had resulted in plans for a 21st Century facility. However, the need was now and the result was nothing less than a miracle. Enter two men of vision, whose impact on the community would be the stuff of which legends are made.

In November 1993, an old Vons grocery store became available at Fairmount Avenue and Landis Street. The City of San Diego was able to negotiate the acquirement of the site, but the problem was —as always—money. Then a 1994 *San Diego Union* article caught two pair of eyes: businessman and philanthropist Sol Price and former City Councilman William Jones. These men had joined forces with a plan to launch a "community-based, entrepreneurial redevelopment project that would marry outside capital to the energy of citizens living within the redevelopment area." After years of planning and "thinking outside of the box," a new police station was born as the centerpiece of this redevelopment.

Chief Jerry Sanders officially opened the Mid-City Police Community Facility in March 1996, with Captain Cliff Resch and a staff of four lieutenants and about 200 police personnel. The impact of this presence can be measured in the steady decline in crime since then.

Police officers in partnership with residents have turned this community around. The Mid-City police station is the centerpiece of an amazing rebirth of the area once again called City Heights.

Credit: San Diego Historical Society

Then and Now

There is an old saying that time changes all things. Certainly, time changes people, needs, desires, and cities. What is often amazing is how quickly change does occur.

The City of East San Diego certainly went through its own changes in its short 11-year history. What may be most remarkable is just how much has been forgotten since that city became part of San Diego. There are, however, a few remnants of that short, bygone era.

One of the most notable changes in ESD was its physical appearance. As original structures grew old and obsolete, they disappeared to be replaced with more "modern" needs. This is especially true with buildings in the business district, as owners constantly change and visions alter. However, in the "historic heart" of old East San Diego, a number of buildings from its incorporated heyday continue to be used, even as they approach their one hundredth anniversary.

Most notably, the Old City Hall is still standing on the northeastern corner of University and Van Dyke Avenues. Slightly altered, it retains some of its original architecture on the east side, facing the east alley. In fact, many of the buildings extent on University Avenue between 42nd and 43rd Streets date from East San Diego. These include:

- The Fairmount Apartments (still apartments as well as a furniture store) on the southwestern corner of 43rd Street and University Avenue
- The Vista Theater (now a store) at the south eastern corner of 42nd Street and University Avenue
- The Bank of East San Diego (now the recently restored Nancy's Pub) and the northwestern corner of Van Dyke and University Avenues.

Additionally, a surprising number of residences throughout the community now known as City Heights date from the days of the old city. Still standing at 37th Street and El Cajon Boulevard is the Hille House, probably the oldest house in the community, dating back to 1889. In fact, this may be the very first house ever in City Heights.

Street names are another oft-altered thing. A 1903 city map shows that University Avenue was once Steiner, Wightman Avenue was Klauber, and Landis Street originally Castle – obviously named after the founders who purchased the land and deemed it "City Heights" back in 1888. Many names changed as the City of East San Diego came into being (1912), and even more changed when the City of San Diego took over in 1923. A major alteration came in 1926, when San Diego changed every other north/south street to a number (commencing with 33rd Street) and, accordingly, realigned the hundred blocks.

Old East San Diego City Hall, 1992

One formerly important road that remains today is Boundary Street. This diagonal (northwest/southeast) street was originally the eastern border of San Diego. But the line predates even San Diego: it was a boundary for the pueblo land grants of old. It served as a starting point for East San Diego and continued as a natural line delineating the community. When Interstate 805 was built and opened in the early 1970's, the freeway became a more natural community border and the significance and even the importance of Boundary Street faded.

Another long forgotten component of the original City Heights was the Park Belt Motor Road. Today, it's hard to believe someone would build a train to City Heights, but that in fact was what occurred back in 1888. Elisha S. Babcock Jr. had come to San Diego in 1884, suffering from tuberculosis and hoping to improve his health. Here he met Hampton L. Story and the two eventually partnered to build the world-famous Hotel Del Coronado. Soon after, they secured a franchise to construct a "steam motor road," seeing the potential of the land boom and the newly formed City Heights community. The line was known by various names, including the very lengthy "City and University Heights Motor Road."

The first train ran on July 6, 1888. Three trains operated on the loop daily, with six stops, three each in both Downtown and City Heights. Fees started at five cents for a trip to the city limits, ten for the City Heights land office, and twenty cents to make the round trip. A small steam engine pulled the cars for most of the journey, switching to the horses of the San Diego Street Car Company while traveling in the Downtown area.

More a railroad than a streetcar, the line commenced in Downtown San Diego at 18th (now part of Interstate 5) and "A" Streets and traveled northeasterly through Switzer canyon, a then far and desolate place. As it reached the area of Boundary and Upas Streets, it looped south down Wabash Canyon, then north once more, and south again to Manzanita Canyon, where it continued northeast and finally climbed onto Marlborough Avenue. What would current residents think to see a railroad car heading north on Marlborough to University Avenue? From there it headed west and finally, at 6th Street, the line turned south and led back into what was then called "New" San Diego.

As the land boom that berthed it went bust, the Park Belt line ran into financial trouble. Sometime in the 1890's, service ended and much of the rails were pulled up and sent elsewhere for use, including San Francisco. There must have been some hope of re-establishing the railway, as a 1903 World Atlas map of San Diego indicated the line and its path. But while streetcars did make it back to East San Diego, the Park Belt Motor Road never

The new Mid-City police station, 2006

reopened. However, as late as 1956, there were reports that residents exploring and hunting in the canyons had come upon some old tracks. One even found an old flatcar. It is unlikely that anything now exists, as the construction of Interstate 805 graded over much of the route in the 1970's.

The community of East San Diego remained fiercely independent for decades, evident by the erection of a community sign in the 1950's, over the intersection of University and Fairmount Avenues. But as the sign came down in 1969, ostensibly to widen University Avenue, the name "East San Diego" took on an evil and negative tone. Many felt a change was needed to make a new start.

There are very few remnants of the old city. They can be hard to find, unless you know where to look. Perhaps the most common may be right under your feet. Many a manhole cover currently in use bears the moniker "Sewerage of East San Diego 1921." These heavy metal lids can be found in some alleys and along much of Orange Avenue, where they will likely continue to be used for years to come.

Most of the original sidewalk stamps have been altered or removed, as streets were either widened or improved. But in at least one place the city has documented an old street with new markers: on the northeast corner of 47th and Landis Street. New concrete was recently laid, indicating the old street "Sierra Avenue" and the original sidewalk company, "JN Chandler 11-6-23."

Following is a list of East San Diego street names—old and new—gathered from a real estate document published in 1926 to assist residence with the new name changed in "Eastern" San Diego, California."

The Streets of East San Diego
North/South Streets
(numbering at University Avenue)

Old Name	Old Block #	New Name	New Block #
1st/Mission N of Univ/36th		33rd	3300
2nd/41st/Pacific	3500	35th	3500
32nd/Illinois	3200	31st	3100
33rd		Iowa	3151
34th/Cliff Place		32nd	3200
35th/Wisconsin		Bancroft	3275
36th/1st/Mission N of Univ		33rd	3300
37th/Boundary	3300	Felton	3351
38th/Scott/Perfect	3400	34th	3400
3rd/45th/Reed	3700	37th	3700
41st/Pacific/2nd	3500	35th	3500
42nd/Wilson	3551	Wilson	3551
43rd/Storey	3600	36th	3600
44th/Bradt	3651	Cherokee	3651
45th/Reed/3rd	3700	37th	3700
46th/Nelson/Thomas	3751	38th	3800
47th/Lafayette/Daley/Rexmore	3800	38th	3900
48th/Sisson/4th	3851	40th	4000
4th/48th/Sisson	3851	40th	4000
5th/Copeland	4051	42nd	4200
Alpine	4700	48th	4800
Boundary/37th	3300	Felton	3351
Bradt/44th	3651	Cherokee	3651
Cabrillo	4351	45th	4500
Central	3900	Central	4051

Cerros	4851	49th	4900
Chamoune	4400	Chamoune	4551
Cliff Place/34th		32nd	3200
Colonial/ Or-angewood	4251	44th	4400
Conklin	3941	41st	4100
Contour Boule-vard		53rd	5300
Copeland/5th	4051	42nd	4200
Daley/Rex-more/ 47th / Lafayette	3800	38th	3900
Estrella	4800	Estrella	4851
Euclid	4600	Euclid	4751
Fairmount		Fairmount	4351
Highland	4300	Highland	4451
Illinois/32nd	3200	31st	3100
Lafayette/Daley/ Rexmore/47th	3800	38th	3900
Lemona		52nd	5200
Manzanita	5000	50th	5000
Menlo	4500	Menlo	4651
Mentone	4451	46th	4600
Mission N of Univ/ 36th/1st		33rd	3300
Mission S of Univ	3351	Nile	3351
Molino		51st	5100
Nelson/Thom-as/ 46th	3751	38th	3800
North Chollas			
Valley Road	.	Chollas	
Orangewood/ Colonial	4251	44th	4400
Pacific /2nd/41st	3500	35th	3500
Pauly	4151	43rd	4300

Prefect/38th/Scott	3400	34th	3400
Radio Road		54th	5400
Reed/3rd/45th	3700	37th	3700
Rexmore/47th/Lafayette/Daley	3800	38th	3900
Scott/Perfect/38th	3400	34th	3400
Sierra	4551	47th	4700
Sisson/4th/48th	3851	40th	4000
Stockton	4000	Marlborough	4151
Storey/43rd	3600	36th	3600
Swift	3451	Swift	3451
Thomas/46th/Nelson	3751	38th	3800
Van Dyke	4100	Van Dyke	4251
Wabash	3357	Wabash	3357
Wilson/42nd	3551	Wilson	3551
Winn		Altadena	5051
Winona	4900	Winona	4951
Wisconsin/35th		Bancroft	3275

East/West Streets

(Numbering South)

Old Name	Old Block #	New Name	New Block #
Mission Drive		Mission Drive	4900
McKinley		Copley	4800
Jefferson		Collier	4700
Adams		Adams	4600
Madison		Madison	4500
Monroe		Monroe	4400
Olive		Meade	4300
El Cajon		El Cajon	4200
Orange		Orange	4100
Anna		Polk	4000
University Avenue		University	3800
Klauber		Wightman	3700
Auburn		Wightman	3700
Castle		Landis	3600
Howard		Dwight	3500
Bowery		Dwight	3500
Clark		Myrtle	3400
Essex		Myrtle	3400
Fulton		Myrtle	3400
Center		Thorn	3200
Kearny		Thorn	3200
Chatham		Redwood	3000
Norfolk		Redwood	3000
Ohio		Quince	2900
Pearl		Quince	2900
Suffolk		Quince	2900

South Of University
East Of Euclid

Old Name		New Name	
Acacia		Reno	
Auburn		Wightman	
South Auburn		Auburn	
Highland		Lantana Drive	
Castle		Landis	
Howard		Dwight	

Lexington Park

Old Name		New Name	
Aaster Street		Cyclamen Street	
Iris Street		Heather Street	
Jasmine Street		Snowdrop Street	
Primrose Street		Tuberose Street	
Pine Street		Laurel Street	
Cypress Street		Arbor Vitae Street	
Manzanita Place		Phlox Street	
Mariposa Street		Modesto Street	
Lilac Street		Sumac Drive	
Orchard Street		Merigold Street	

Courtesy of E.W. Dickenson, Real Estate/Loans/Notary, 4332 (formerly 4182) University Avenue (Next to Tower) Hillcrest 990-W, East San Diego, Calif. (Circa 1926)

Appendix A

Personnel of the East San Diego Police Department, 1912-1923

CHIEFS OF POLICE/CITY MARSHALS

Charles W. Justice ... Nov 1912 – Feb 1913
Frank A. Hyatt ... Mar 1913 – Jun 1914
James P. Ayers ... Jun 1914 – Apr 1915
Austin R. Cole ... Apr 1915 – Apr 1916
James P. Ayers ... Apr 1916 – May 1918
William H. Gray ... May 1918 – Jun 1922
William Martin, *Acting* ... Dec 1920 – Mar 1921
Nathaniel J. McHorney Jr ... Jun 1922 – Dec 1923

CONSTABLES

Harold J. Slease, constable ... 1913
Charles F. Rapp, deputy constable ... 1915
Charles E. Murray, constable ... 1914 – 1918
William M. Tompkins, chief deputy constable ... 1916

CITY MARSHALS, DEPUTIES, OTHER EMPLOYEES

Marshal	**Charles W. Justice**

Marshal	**Frank A. Hyatt**
Deputy Marshals:	George A. DeBarrow
	R.L. Green
	James Holgate
Deputy Tax Collector:	Bessie Seay

Marshal	**James P. Ayers**
Deputy Marshal:	J.R. Davis

Marshal	**Austin R. Cole**
Deputy Marshal:	Frank A. Hyatt

Marshal	**James P. Ayers**
Deputy Marshals:	Paul Ford
	Frank A. Hyatt
	Silas Puryear

Marshal	**William H. Gray**
Deputy Marshals:	Roy O. Akers
	B. Curtis
	Lester Davis
	E.W. Dickenson
	Edward B. Hare
	George F. "Buck" Hyatt
	Jay Matthews
	J.B. Michael
	O.H. Mills
	August "Gus" Nachant

Al Olson
John P. Roberts
John Schertzinger
E.R. Slinkard
Motorcycle /Traffic: Howard S. Fraser
Howard W. Jack
William L. Martin
Night Policemen: Pat Shannon
C.E. Murray
Nat McHorney
Auto Hire: Joseph Carter
Special Services: R.V. Green
Interpreter: Mrs. Sista Martinez
Timing Speeders: Arthur Tocque
Acting Marshal: William L. Martin

Marshal   **Nathaniel J. McHorney Jr.**
Deputy Marshals: Howard Jack
P.G. Kerr, Jr.
Traffic: Edward Moore, Jr.